MORTGAGE
&SECRETS
STRATEGIES
WARNINGS

INSIDE INFORMATION ON HOW TO SAVE THOUSANDS ON YOUR MORTGAGE.

JEFF FLEES

MARALA SCOTT

I strongly recommend that you read *Mortgage Secrets, Strategies, & Warnings* for yourself and pass this information along as a parent, mentor, or advisor to our young people. It is necessary for them to be prepared to make better financial decisions in their lifetime.

–Marala Scott

Cover Design: Alyssa M. Curry
Cover Photo: Andreas Braun
Copy Editing: Alyssa M. Curry
ISBN Hardcover: 978-1-941711-12-5
ISBN Paperback: 978-1-941711-13-2
ISBN E-book: 978-1-941711-14-9
Library of Congress Control Number: 2014922301

For information regarding special discounts for bulk purchases of this book for educational or gift purposes, as a charitable donation, or to arrange a speaking event with the authors, please contact Seraph Books. www.seraphbooks.com

Jeff Flees

Twitter: https://twitter.com/JeffFlees
Facebook: https://www.facebook.com/jeff.flees
LinkedIn: https://www.linkedin.com/pub/jeff-flees/11/409/786

Marala Scott

Twitter: https://twitter.com/maralascott
Facebook: https://www.facebook.com/marala.scott
LinkedIn: www.linkedin.com/pub/marala-scott/b/718/127

Table of Contents

Dedication vii
Introduction viii

CHAPTER 1: FUNDAMENTALS TO BORROWING
MONEY 1

Continue to Make All Your Current Payments on Time 2
Do Not Pay Upfront Application Fees 4
Improve Your Credit Score Before You Apply For a Loan 5
Minimize Credit Inquiries 7
Borrow Only What You Need 8
When Possible, Choose the Shorter Term 9
Have Your Financial Documents Readily Available 10
Make Sure You Have the Ability
to Repay the Loan Applied For 11
Protect Your Identity 12
If You Co-sign on a Loan, Expect to Make the Payments 15

CHAPTER 2: UNDERSTANDING YOUR CREDIT
REPORT AND HOW TO IMPROVE YOUR SCORE 17

Factors That Affect Credit Scores 18
What is Included in Your Credit Report? 20
How to Obtain a Free Copy and
Dispute Errors in Your Credit Report 21
Strategies to Improve Your Credit Score 24
Protecting Your Privacy and Identity Theft 27
Bankruptcy and Negative
Information on Credit Reports 30
Primary Laws That Protect Consumers
in Mortgage Transactions 34
Frequently Asked Questions
About Credit and Credit Scores 37

CHAPTER 3: HOW THE MORTGAGE APPLICATION WORKS 45

Trust and Transparency 46

CHAPTER 4: UNDERSTANDING UNDERWRITING STANDARDS 83

CHAPTER 5: ADDITIONAL MORTGAGE OPTIONS 97

CHAPTER 6: **STRATEGIES** TO NEGOTIATING A GREAT MORTGAGE 109

CHAPTER 7: **SECRETS** LENDERS AND LOAN OFFICERS DON'T WANT YOU TO KNOW................... 117

CHAPTER 8: **WARNINGS!** HOW TO AVOID SURPRISES AND BE PREPARED FOR WHAT CAN GO WRONG 125

About the Authors 137

DEDICATION

This book is dedicated to my mother. Your love, work ethic, and character are remarkable and helped shape me into the person I am today.

Additionally, this book is dedicated to my wife. Your love, support, and inspiration are truly amazing and appreciated. You are a gift from God.

INTRODUCTION

The purpose of this book is to provide individuals with the knowledge and strategies essential to obtain an excellent rate and low cost mortgage. We will help you avoid many of the most common mistakes made and give you inside information that a mortgage professional or lender may not share with you. After practicing these strategies, never again will you say, "I wish I would have known," when applying for or obtaining a new mortgage. Instead you will say, "Wow! That was faster, simpler, and less stressful than I expected!" You will be armed with knowledge regarding the process.

While the lending marketplace and how we obtain a mortgage is constantly evolving, there are fundamentals that you should know and apply throughout your lifetime. These basics pertain to most loans and will save thousands of dollars if you follow them. We will share these fundamentals in **CHAPTER 1: FUNDAMENTALS TO BORROWING MONEY** and build from there.

Your credit history and score are critical when applying for a mortgage. Don't wait until you decide to purchase a home or refinance your current mortgage to pay attention to what is in your report. Request a free copy of your report annually or three to six months prior to making a loan application. Then, follow the information in **CHAPTER 2: UNDERSTANDING YOUR CREDIT REPORT AND HOW TO IMPROVE YOUR SCORE** to make the changes necessary to improve your credit score.

Applying for a mortgage can be overwhelming. How do you know where to begin and who to trust?

In **CHAPTER 3: HOW THE MORTGAGE APPLICATION PROCESS WORKS**, we guide you through the application process and let you know what to expect. We answer the most important questions so that you will be prepared and confident when you are applying for a new mortgage. Underwriting practices and guidelines can be complicated and change with market conditions. In **CHAPTER 4: UNDERSTANDING UNDERWRITING STANDARDS**, we provide you with the fundamentals to mortgage underwriting and strategies on how to qualify for the best mortgage. We want you to know when someone is misleading or trying to take advantage of you.

While the majority of mortgage loans are closed using a forward first mortgage, there are other products in the marketplace. In **CHAPTER 5: ADDITIONAL MORTGAGE OPTIONS**, we share the alternative mortgages that are available to you. We will explain the benefits and risks of these loan programs.

Most of the time, it's not what you know that gets you in trouble, it's what you don't. *Mortgage Secrets, Strategies, & Warnings* will provide you with the truth and transparency of how the mortgage industry works. In **CHAPTER 6: STRATEGIES TO NEGOTIATING A GREAT MORTGAGE**, we provide additional inside information and strategies you should follow.

Throughout this book, we will incorporate real life scenarios and decisions you will need to make. We dispel some aggressive sales strategies and warn you about things others would prefer that you don't know. In **CHAPTER 7: SECRETS LENDERS AND LOAN OFFICERS DON'T WANT YOU TO KNOW**, we share many of the secrets within the mortgage industry.

There are many moving parts and things that can go wrong when you apply for a mortgage. Some of these items will cause your loan application to be declined. Throughout the book and in **CHAPTER 8: WARNINGS! HOW TO AVOID SURPRISES AND BE PREPARED FOR WHAT CAN GO WRONG**, we convey warnings you will want to know about. These warnings are meant to raise red flags in regards to what could go wrong with your application or when an originator is being less than truthful. Working with someone that is willing to be transparent about his or her objectives is important. The goal is to help you avoid surprises and close your mortgage in a timely manner at the best terms.

Knowledge is powerful when negotiating a mortgage and making financial decisions. It is important to have accurate information as it can positively change your life. While the focus of this book is the mortgage marketplace, we're optimistic that you will apply the lessons learned to many of the financial decisions and loans you will obtain throughout your lifetime. We want you to be fearless, stress-free, and save thousands of dollars when borrowing money.

—1—

TOP TEN FUNDAMENTALS TO BORROWING MONEY

When you make the decision to borrow money, there are several things you'll want to know in order to make the best financial decision and to protect yourself from unscrupulous individuals and lenders. Too often, people apply for a mortgage without understanding what they are doing and how their premature actions can hurt them. The list below is our top ten fundamentals or basic rules to follow so that you will get your loan funded quicker and with better terms.

1. Continue to make all of your current payments on time.
2. Do not pay upfront fees.

3. Improve your credit score before you apply for a loan.
4. Minimize credit inquiries.
5. Borrow only what you need.
6. When possible, choose the shorter term.
7. Have your financial documents readily available.
8. Make sure you have the ability to repay the loan applied for.
9. Protect your identity.
10. If you co-sign on a loan, expect to make the payments.

CONTINUE TO MAKE ALL YOUR CURRENT PAYMENTS ON TIME

When you are applying for a new loan, it is important that you continue to make all of your existing payments as required. While the application process to obtain a personal or auto loan can take hours or days, mortgage applications take weeks or even months to close. Lenders often pull an updated credit report the day before closing and if your credit score has dropped, there is new debt, or they see a late payment on the credit report, they may decline your previously approved loan.

Warning: Mortgage applications don't always close on time and plans can go extremely wrong. When applying for a mortgage, borrowers often believe or are told by their loan officer/originator that they can skip making their payment because the new loan will close before the existing loan is past due.

Truth: Mortgage payments are due on the 1st of the month but on the 15th, they are considered late.

Payments do not show up as late on your credit report until you are 30 days late. However, on the 16th, you will incur late fees.

Real life scenario: There are so many moving parts that need to be coordinated and factors that can cause a mortgage not to close in a timely manner that are beyond the borrower or loan originator's control. For example, the appraisal may show repairs that need to be made prior to closing. The property's appraised value is lower than what is needed to complete the refinance or purchase. Your loan may be delayed in underwriting waiting for required documentation. Additionally, there may be issues on the properties title, with an existing payoff, or something as unexpected as a major storm may postpone the closing. If you skip your existing payment and the new mortgage does not fund by the 30th, the underwriter may decline your application. This new late payment may keep you from being able to refinance at the best possible rate and terms. Additionally, you will have a late payment show up on your credit report that will drop your credit score, hurt your ability to borrow for other loans, and it may increase the interest rates on your credit cards or insurance premiums. Do not put yourself in this position; make sure you continue to pay all your bills.

Time is nothing to make light of when it comes to handling your business. Being ill-advised can hurt your next move.

DO NOT PAY UPFRONT APPLICATION FEES

Reputable lenders, brokers, and mortgage professionals do not charge individuals upfront application fees in order to quote you a rate or provide you with a mortgage proposal.

Warning: If the website, individual, or company you are working with requires you to pay an upfront application fee, stop your application and find another source. Additionally, you may want to report the party to the Better Business Bureau, the appropriate state agency that oversees the mortgage company or lender, and the Attorney General's office.

Truth: Many times the application fees are the sole source of revenue for phantom companies. Once they have your funds, it may be difficult to contact them again. Other times, the website operator, broker, and lender may be licensed to provide mortgage services for you. However, they may lack the professional ability or loan products to properly meet your needs and find it easier to charge application fees.

Real life scenario: Competition from various lenders, brokers, and mortgage professionals has created an environment where borrowers can review loan proposals and apply for a mortgage without paying an upfront application fee. In fact, when you make an application and are quoted an interest rate, you are legally required to be presented with a good faith estimate (GFE) detailing what the associated fees for the new loan are, and the corresponding Annual Percentage Rate (APR). APR's can be confusing to borrowers as they differ from the interest rates. APR's take into account the fees involved in the loan and are intended to allow borrowers to comparison shop between loan offers. The lower the APR, the better it is for the borrower, if the loan program is the same.

IMPROVE YOUR CREDIT SCORE BEFORE YOU APPLY FOR A LOAN

Your credit profile and score are critical in the mortgage process. With a higher credit score, you will have an easier time getting approved and obtaining a loan with lower interest rates and fees.

Because this is such an important area we have dedicated a complete chapter to this topic. However, the main point we want you to understand, is that you should improve your credit score before applying for a mortgage, not after. Improving your score is not a quick fix; rather it is a continuous process. The major factors involved in your credit score are how you pay your obligations, the length of time you've paid your credit, the percentage of credit you are using, and the different types of credit you have.

Strategy: The first thing you should do is to obtain a copy of your credit report and review it for any incorrect information or inconsistencies.

A simple error that isn't yours can cost you. Take caution in reviewing your credit report.

Every person is legally entitled to a free copy annually by going to www.annualcreditreport.com. While this report will not give you a score, it will provide the information that is showing on the three main reporting agencies, Equifax, Experian, and

5

Trans Union. If you want a report with a score, you can go directly to the credit reporting agencies website; however, you may have to pay a fee. Additional websites and companies might provide a free credit report with a score but they are not a direct source and will market other products and services to you. Review the report for any errors and dispute anything that is inaccurate. We will explain how to dispute these items later in the chapter on credit.

The other **strategies** to improve your credit score are:

1. Pay all of your bills on time. If you missed a payment(s), get current and stay up-to-date.
2. Keep balances low. Having a balance that is less than 30% of the high credit limit demonstrates financial responsibility. When your balance is more than 50%, red flags start to go up and the credit score goes down. Having a balance greater than the high credit limit will crush a credit score. When credit is maxed out, the risk of default is much higher.
3. Have different types of credit. For example, having two installment loans (mortgage, auto, student) and two revolving loans (credit cards) is better than having two secured revolving accounts.
4. Minimize "hard" inquiries and opening new accounts that are not necessary. The longer the accounts are open, the better the score. New accounts show additional risk and will lower your score.

MINIMIZE CREDIT INQUIRIES

Hard inquiries are the result of applying for a new loan, credit card, or other financial related products or services, such as a rental application from a third party. Hard inquiries lower your credit score a few points because there is additional risk when you take on new debt or financial responsibilities. Inquiries stay on your report for two years, however those inquiries within the last twelve months affect your score. Additionally, many lenders will require an explanation for any recent inquiries and proof that you haven't taken on new debt. If you have, the lender will require documentation on the debt and use this information in underwriting your loan file.

Soft inquiries are when you obtain a copy of your credit report or when financial institutions review the credit scores and profiles of current or potential clients without a hard inquiry. Financial institutions often use soft inquiries to review the customers who they have issued credit cards to. Since most credit cards are unsecured, if your score has dropped, the bank may increase the rate, lower the credit limit, or cancel the card completely. When you or a financial institution completes a soft inquiry, this does not show up as an inquiry on your credit report or affect your credit score.

Question: You are shopping for a new car loan or mortgage and apply with multiple lenders or originators in a short period of time who all pull your credit. Will this significantly lower your credit score because of multiple inquiries?

Answer: Multiple inquiries within a short period of time by companies in the same industry, like mortgages and auto loans, are treated as one inquiry by most credit scoring models. All of the inquiries will show up on your credit report but will be treated as one inquiry and have minimal affect on the credit score. Applying for multiple credit cards will be treated as separate inquiries as each new debt equates to additional risk.

BORROW ONLY WHAT YOU NEED

Just because you qualify for a $100,000 car or $500,000 home, doesn't mean you should buy them. The added risk for a higher loan may result in a higher interest rate. Furthermore, the large payment could jeopardize your budget, financial situation, and ability to obtain future loans.

Real life scenario: Often, the first major purchase college graduates make when they get a full-time job is a car. They purchase a new upscale vehicle that comes with a monthly payment between $650-$700 for the next 60 months. Add this to their student loans and credit card balances and they are living the American Dream of being in debt. A year or two later, they get married and want to purchase a new home. This is where the previous decisions catch up with the graduate. They haven't been able to save money for the down payment, their credit scores are marginal, and their debt ratio is too high to buy the home they want.

> Just because you want it, doesn't make it a wise decision. It is best to make decisions that coincide with your reality.

Remember it is important to have a plan when borrowing money. The decisions you make today will affect what you can do in the future. A better plan would have been to buy a car with a lower payment and then utilize the additional funds to pay off the credit card debt and save for a down payment. The result would be higher credit scores and lower debt ratio. When they apply for the home loan, they will have numerous mortgage options and can get approved for a loan at the best rates in the marketplace.

WHEN POSSIBLE, CHOOSE THE SHORTER TERM

When you choose a shorter term, the interest rate is usually lower as the risk of default is less for the lender. More importantly, the total interest you pay back to the lender is much lower. Remember, your payments will be higher with a shorter term and you need to plan accordingly. If you are concerned about your ability to make the larger payments, go with the longer term. If you have future borrowing needs, consider how the larger payments will affect your debt ratio and ability to get approved.

Real life scenario: You are buying a home and interested in obtaining a mortgage loan for $200,000. You want a fixed rate and decide to compare the rates and payments between the two most popular terms, 30 and 15 years. Rates on a 30-year term are traditionally .50-1.0% higher than a 15-year term. For comparison purposes, the sample rate for a 30-year fixed is 5% and a 15-year fixed is 4.25%.

The payment on the 30-year loan is $1,073.64 and the total of all your payments is $386,511. For the 15-year loan, the payment is $1,504.55 and the total payment is $270,820. While your payments are $430.91 higher on a 15-year loan, if you paid each loan as agreed for the entire term, you would pay back $115,691 less in interest to the lender for the 15-year term.

While a longer term may allow for lower monthly payments that are easier to make, borrowing money for a shorter term will save you money over the life of a loan.

HAVE YOUR FINANCIAL DOCUMENTS READILY AVAILABLE

Lenders are required to make sure you have the ability to repay the mortgage you are applying for. This is accomplished by reviewing your income and assets in the underwriting process. Before you apply, you should put together income documentation from the last two years. If you are a W-2'd employee, this would be your two most recent pay stubs and last two years of W-2's. If you are self-employed or receive a 1099, put together a recent profit and loss or income statement along with your last two years tax returns.

If your income is derived from sources like Social Security, child support, alimony, pensions, or worker's compensation, have your award letter(s) along with your last three bank statements showing the applicable deposit available. Lenders will want to make sure your income is going to continue for a minimum of three years with these alternative income sources.

When verifying your assets, you should have your last three bank statements and most recent investment and retirement statements available.

Please note that if your bank statements show NSF (non-sufficient funds) charges, your likelihood for approval will be diminished greatly.

The additional documentation you may be asked for may include: a copy of your driver's license, Social Security card, divorce decree, copy of your diploma, incorporation papers if you are a business, copy of the HUD-1 and Note from your last mortgage closing, current mortgage statement(s), and a copy of your homeowner's insurance policy.

While the documentation needed will be different for various loan types, how quickly your loan closes is largely determined by how timely you provide the lender or originator with the required documentation.

Providing false or misleading information on a loan application or in the supplemental documentation is fraud. Do not try to outsmart the lender, as you will get caught. Technology easily verifies everything in a loan file and underwriters will automatically decline the loan and may report you to the appropriate agencies.

MAKE SURE YOU HAVE THE ABILITY TO REPAY THE LOAN APPLIED FOR

Do not take on a new mortgage or more debt than you can afford to pay back. Lenders are required to review your income and ability to repay the loan in the underwriting process. However, withholding information or intentionally misleading your lender about a pending divorce, medical situation, loss or change in employment, lost business contract, or other situation that may result in you defaulting on your loan is a serious problem for everyone involved in the transaction.

Additionally, when you complete a loan application, you are legally required to disclose all of your current debts and the loans that you have applied for, not simply what shows up on your credit report. While you may not have intended to misrepresent yourself, failure to disclose a new debt is fraudulent and may have serious consequences.

For example, if you are looking to buy a new home, do not buy a new car or open a credit card and buy home furnishings while your loan is in underwriting. Doing so would require you to disclose this to your lender and they will need to re-underwrite your loan. This could slow down your approval process or cause your loan to be declined. This is because your credit score may have dropped and no longer meets the minimum requirements or your debt ratio (the percentage of debt you have in relation to your income) may now be too high.

PROTECT YOUR IDENTITY

When you are looking to obtain a new mortgage, I strongly urge you to be careful about revealing your Social Security number, driver's license number, bank accounts, credit card numbers, or other confidential information online or to your originator until you are ready. Make sure you are working with a

> Don't disclose personal information online that can cause identity theft. Just because you are asked for it doesn't mean you should provide it.

reputable company that has well-defined privacy policies and procedures in place. Furthermore, be advised as to how the financial institution is going to use your information and only provide them with what they need. For instance, if your lender doesn't need your credit card numbers or spouse's Social Security number, do not offer it.

We'd recommend that you work with a company that will provide you with a valid quote without divulging confidential information. Once you are comfortable with what they offer, then proceed with sharing your Social Security number and financial documents.

Warning: Many people go to the Internet to search for mortgage information and the best rates, however, they do not understand the consequences. Have you ever filled out a loan application online with only one company and wonder why you are now being called and emailed by over 20 different lenders or brokers?

What happened is that you completed an application with a marketing company, not a lender, banker, or broker. These companies advertise extremely low rates, often, below market or for adjustable rate mortgages. When you complete their application, your information is sold to lenders, mortgage bankers, and/or brokers. Most marketing companies sell your application four to six different times. Some of those who purchase the "Internet leads" will later resell them.

While competition from multiple lenders and brokers may result in you obtaining a mortgage with lower interest rates and fees, do not work with services that require you to provide a Social Security number to obtain a rate quote. There is added risk of identity theft as they gather your information and sell it multiple times.

If you are concerned about your private information being stolen, known as identity theft, immediately request a copy of your credit report (explained in, Improve Your Credit Score Before You Apply for a Loan) and check it for accuracy. Depending on your situation, you may want to sign up for a credit monitoring service. If your confidential information was compromised through a security breach at a financial institution or retail business, they typically will pay for the credit monitoring service. Then contact all of your credit and debit card providers to inform them of your concerns and ask them to replace that card with a new card. Additionally, you can protect yourself by changing your passwords. Always shred unwanted financial documents and credit card statements. When discarding an old computer make sure you delete confidential personal information from the hard drive.

Experience and ethics do matter. The lowest advertised rate is not always the best solution for you. In addition to the rates advertised online being misleading, inexperienced originators often work the Internet leads. Typically, experienced originators have established referral sources and clients. You can check out the loan originator's license status and experience. Visit www.nmlsconsumeraccess.org. Additionally, you can review the Better Business Bureau and other online rating companies that share more information about the company or individual you are considering working with.

IF YOU CO-SIGN ON A LOAN, EXPECT TO MAKE THE PAYMENTS

Co-signers are individuals who are added to a loan application because their strong credit, income, and asset profile will help the primary borrower get approved for a loan. There is minimal financial benefit to the co-signer. The debt will show up on your credit profile and could hurt your ability to get a mortgage in the future. Additionally, if the primary borrower does not make the payment, you are required to or you will also incur a blemish on your credit report. Historically, more than half of the time, the co-signer ends up making the loan payments. Therefore, co-signing for a loan should be done with extreme caution. The negatives, financially and emotionally usually outweigh the benefits.

Real life scenario: The number of mortgage applications that we've seen declined because a parent co-signed for an auto or student loan is unbelievable. It is really sad because the child didn't make the parent aware of the missed payment(s). The parent found out when they applied for a loan to purchase a new home or refinance an existing mortgage. At this point, it is too late. Their credit score has dropped significantly and the mortgage application is declined. The parent then scrambles to get the bad loan and all the late fees and penalties resolved, only to find that they have to wait for months or years to rebuild their credit score and profile.

Loving someone doesn't mean giving them everything they ask for, especially if it isn't teaching them financial responsibility.

—2—

UNDERSTANDING YOUR CREDIT REPORT AND IMPROVING YOUR SCORE

Your credit profile and score are critical to borrowing money, getting approved for a credit card, obtaining insurance, or when applying for a job. With a higher credit score, you will have an easier time accessing credit and obtaining a loan with lower interest rates and fees. It will be easier to obtain home and auto insurance at the lowest premiums. Plus, a strong credit profile may be the difference as to whether or not you get hired for employment. Credit scores help lenders, insurers, employers and financial

Your knowledge is power so use it wisely.

institutions measure consumer risk, which predicts the future credit behavior and stability of an applicant.

FACTORS THAT AFFECT CREDIT SCORES

In order to help you understand how to improve your score, let's start by explaining what factors affect your credit score as outlined by Fair Isaac Corporation (FICO). FICO created the initial credit scoring model and system that is widely accepted and required by most lenders and financial institutions in the United States.

1. Payment history (35%)
2. Amount owed (30%)
3. Length of credit history (15%)
4. Type of credit (10%)
5. Number of inquiries and new debt (10%)

Payment history (35%): The first thing the lender wants to know is how you have paid your previous obligations. There are many different types of accounts that are included:

- Mortgage loans
- Credit cards (Visa, MasterCard, American Express, Discover, etc.)
- Installment loans (auto, student, personal)
- Retail accounts (department store credit)
- Finance company credit

The type of account and how many accounts you have open and paid as agreed will affect your score. Major accounts open for longer periods of time will positively affect your score more than minor accounts or major accounts open for a short time.

Public records and non-medical collection accounts are serious and negatively affect your score. Older items and smaller amounts will have less impact on your score than more recent items and larger accounts. Negative items and delinquencies include: bankruptcies, liens, collections, charge offs, foreclosures, lawsuits, and judgments.

Amount owed (30%): This addresses how much of your available credit limits you are currently using and how many accounts have balances. Keeping your utilization rate below 30% is considered ideal. When your utilization rate is over 50% and you have balances on multiple accounts, the risk of you being overextended will cause your credit score to go down. Older installment loans paid as agreed will help your score more than new loans that have a large balance relative to the original loan amount.

Length of credit history (15%): How long your credit accounts have been open will impact your credit score. This includes your oldest account, newest account, and the average age of all your accounts. Additionally, this takes into consideration how long it has been since you've used an account. Generally speaking, it is not a good idea to close a credit card or line of credit that you have had for a long period of time, even if it has a zero balance and you don't need it.

Type of credit (10%): Having a variety of accounts, mortgages, credit cards, installment loans, retail accounts, or finance company credit and paying them as agreed shows that you can handle all types of debt. Having credit cards and managing them effectively shows you are more responsible than an individual who doesn't have any credit cards. Lenders prefer clients that have a track record of paying three or more different accounts.

Number of inquiries and new debt (10%): Hard inquiries are the result of applying for a new loan, credit card, or other financial related products or services, such as a rental application, from a third party. Hard inquiries lower your credit score a few points because there is additional risk in you taking on new debt or financial responsibilities. Inquiries stay on your report for two years, however those inquiries within the last twelve months affect your score. Soft inquiries are when you or an existing creditor pulls your credit. Soft inquiries do not affect your credit score.

Multiple inquiries within a short period of time by companies in the same industry, such as mortgage and auto lending, are treated as one inquiry by most credit scoring models. This is not the same for credit cards, where multiple inquiries equate to added risk that the consumer is about to take on new debt and may become financially challenged.

WHAT IS INCLUDED IN YOUR CREDIT REPORT?

While each of the credit reporting agencies, Equifax, Experian, and Trans Union may format the material differently, all credit reports have the same basic information.

Identifying information: This includes your name, previous and current addresses, phone number, Social Security number, date of birth, as well as previous and current employment. This information does not affect your credit score.

Trade lines: These are your previous and current credit accounts within the last seven years. Each lender or creditor will provide specific information, such as the date opened, credit limit or loan amount, balance, monthly payment, type of account, and payment history.

Credit inquiries: This is a list of every company that has pulled your credit within the last two years and the date of the inquiry.

Public record and collection items: This includes public record information from state and county courts along with collection agencies.

HOW TO OBTAIN A FREE COPY AND DISPUTE ERRORS IN YOUR CREDIT REPORT

Every person is legally entitled to a free copy of his or her credit report annually by visiting www.annualcreditreport.com, writing to Annual Credit Report, P.O. Box 105281 Atlanta, GA 30348-5281, or by calling (877) 322-8228. While this report will not give you a score, it will provide the information that is showing on the three main credit reporting agencies. If you want a report with a score, go directly to a credit reporting agencies website; however, you may have to pay a fee.

When reviewing the report, make sure you review everything, which includes personal information, trade lines, credit inquiries, public records, and collection items. Many errors exist because the information hasn't been updated, data was input incorrectly, payments were applied to wrong accounts, or the credit is applicable to another person. Pay close attention to the following:

- **Trade lines:** Make sure your payment history is accurate. Don't overlook what the report states as your high credit limit for each account. For example, if you have a credit card with a high credit limit of $5,000 and a balance of $600, but the report states the credit limit is $500. Your credit score will be 20 to 60 points lower than it should be because it appears that you are over your high credit limit, when you actually owe less than 15% of the high credit.
- **Public records and collection items:** There are many errors in this section as accounts are often sold and not updated when satisfied, especially after a bankruptcy.
- **Personal information:** Errors often result when you have a common name, changed names through marriage, or have family members with the same name.
- **Inquiries:** Make sure your credit profile hasn't been accessed without your knowledge or consent. This can be a sign you are at risk for identity theft.

If there are errors, the fastest and easiest solution to fix the problem is to follow the dispute procedures on the credit reporting agencies website. If you report an error to a credit reporting agency, they must investigate and respond to you within 30 days or they will be violating the law and subject to fines and disciplinary actions. In addition, if you are in the process of applying for a loan, immediately notify your lender of any incorrect information in your report. The contact information for the credit reporting agencies dispute departments is:

Equifax: (866) 238-8067
https://www.ai.equifax.com/CreditInvestigation/home.action.
Mail disputes to: Equifax Disputes, P.O. Box 740256, Atlanta, GA 30374-0256

Experian: (formerly TRW): (888) 397-3742
http://www.experian.com/disputes/main.html.
Mail disputes to: Experian Disputes, P.O. Box 4500, Allen, TX 75013.

TransUnion: (800) 916-8800
https://dispute.transunion.com.
Mail disputes to: TransUnion Disputes, 2 Baldwin Place, P.O. Box 1000, Chester, PA 19022.

When you file for a dispute, make sure to provide any supporting information you have. The credit reporting agency will contact the source of the information and one of three things will happen:

- Incorrect information will be corrected.
- Information that cannot be verified will be updated or deleted.
- Information verified as accurate will remain intact on your credit report.

This process can take up to 60 days, however it usually is updated in less than 30 days. The credit reporting agency will contact you with the results of their investigation.

Please be aware that if you file a dispute with one credit reporting agency, it does not update the other two bureaus. These are independent companies who do not share data. You must file a dispute with each credit reporting agency to correct information on all three of your credit reports.

In the event you are denied credit, the Equal Credit Opportunity Act (ECOA) requires the creditor to inform you as well as provide the reasons for the denial within 30 days of the initial application. If this happens, make sure you obtain a copy of your credit report and review it for errors.

We strongly encourage you to follow the dispute procedures outlined above. If the process intimidates or aggravates you, there are companies that will repair your credit for a fee, usually between $500 and $2,000. The Credit Repair Organizations Act regulates credit repair or restoration companies. Make sure the company is appropriately licensed and doesn't have complaints filed against them. While these companies may be experienced and provide excellent advice, there isn't a quick fix they can do that you can't do yourself. An individual or company cannot force a creditor or credit reporting agency to delete or remove accurate information from your account. In most cases, you and your credit score would be better off by using the $500 to $2,000 to pay down credit card balances, other debt, or open a secured credit card.

STRATEGIES TO IMPROVE YOUR CREDIT SCORE

There isn't a quick fix to improving your credit score. Time and managing your credit responsibly are required. Having a plan and committing to it will determine how high your credit score can get and how much money you will save by doing so.

1. The first thing you should do is obtain a copy of your credit report and review it for any incorrect information or inconsistencies. Ideally, you should check your credit, three to six months, before applying for a loan or insurance so you have time to have errors corrected.
2. Pay all of your bills on time. If you missed a payment(s), get current and stay up-to-date. Additionally, you can set up your accounts with payment reminders or automatic withdrawals from your bank account.
3. Keep balances and utilization rates low. Make it a priority to pay down accounts that are closest to their credit limits first. Having a balance that is less than 30% of the high credit limit demonstrates financial responsibility. When your balance is more than 50%, red flags start to go up and the credit score goes down. Having a balance greater than the high credit limit will crush a credit score. When credit is maxed out, the risk of default is much higher.
4. Have different types of credit. For example, having two installment loans (mortgage, auto, student, personal) and two revolving loans (credit cards or retail accounts) is better than having two unsecured revolving accounts.
5. Minimize "hard" inquiries and opening new accounts that are not necessary. The longer the accounts are open, the better the score. New accounts show additional risk and will lower your score.
6. Pay off collections or charge offs except when you are planning a new loan. Paying off an old

negative account becomes a recent delinquent activity causing your scores to go lower in the short term then it will rise over time.

7. Establishing credit when you are young or re-establishing credit after a challenging financial period is important and requires discipline. Credit cards are a great place to start, even if it has to be a secured card. Secured cards are designed for people with no credit history or with current or past credit problems. The credit limit is "secured" by a security deposit made by the consumer into a FDIC insured bank account. Your payment history is reported to the three credit reporting agencies just like any other credit card. Whether you obtain a traditional credit card or a secured credit card, it is important to never miss a payment and to keep balances low or paid off each month.

A strong credit score can save you thousands of dollars. It will give you access to the best interest rates when you apply for a mortgage, qualify you for more loan programs, provide access to the best credit cards, and lower premiums on your insurance policies.

The table below is a historical average on delinquency rates associated with a specific credit score range through Fair Isaac Corporation (FICO) the company that created the first credit scoring model. FICO scores range between 300 and 850 and is the primary scoring model used by most lenders and financial institutions to assess the risk. Underwriters, especially in the mortgage and insurance industries, take this into account when deciding whether or not to approve an applicant and in the rate that is offered. For example, if the applicant's credit score is between 550-599, one out of every two clients will become delinquent in their payments. Whereas, on average when the credit score is between 700-749, one out of twenty clients will become delinquent in their payments.

Historical Average on Delinquency Rates and FICO Scores

Percentile	% Of People	Score	Delinquency Rate
2nd	2%	300-499	87%
7th	5%	500-549	71%
15th	8%	550-599	51%
27th	12%	600-649	31%
42nd	15%	650-699	15%
60th	18%	700-749	5%
87th	27%	750-799	2%
100th	13%	800-850	1%

PROTECTING YOUR PRIVACY AND IDENTITY THEFT

In order to maintain a strong credit score, you need to protect your personal and financial information. Following the tips below will help protect your privacy and reduce the possibility of identity theft.

- Do not send your Social Security number, credit card account numbers, or bank account information in an email.

- Keep financial information, Social Security card, checks, and credit cards in a safe place. Do not carry your Social Security card with you.
- Shred all documents and statements when you no longer need them. Do not throw them in the trash.
- When applying for a loan, do not provide your Social Security number and financial account information until it is absolutely necessary.
- When you send financial documents or loan applications with personal information that includes your Social Security number, use a secure email system or password protect the documents.
- When replacing personal computers, mobile phones, servers, or other IT equipment, remove all personal information and have them properly sanitized before disposing.

Identity theft is when someone steals and uses your personal or financial information for their financial gain. Often, thieves make purchases with your credit cards, open new bank, cellular, and credit accounts in your name, or take out loans for a major purchase such as a car. By checking your credit report annually, you can make sure there isn't anything on the report that you didn't authorize. If you believe that your personal information has been stolen and used illegally, take action immediately.

The following actions are recommended in most cases:

- Call the fraud department at any one of the

three major credit reporting agencies and place a fraud alert on your credit report. When you do this, a fraud alert for 90 days will be placed on all three reports. Any requested change in your credit or opening of a new account will take additional verification directly from you. You can extend the 90-day fraud alert on your credit profile to seven years if you provide a police report verifying you were a victim of identity theft.

- Contact the lender(s) or creditor(s) and close any accounts that have been tampered with or opened fraudulently. Ask them to stop reporting any derogatory information to the credit reporting agencies. Then ask the creditor to issue replacement cards with new account numbers.
- Monitor your credit report on a regular basis. When identity theft resulted from a security breach of a third party, such as a lender or retail store, they traditionally pay for a credit monitoring service.
- File a police report where you live or in the community where the identity theft happened.
- File a complaint with the Federal Trade Commission. The identity theft hotline is:

(877) 438-4338 or
www.ftc.gov/bcp/edu/microsites/idtheft

- Keep excellent records. Recovering from identity theft can be a long and difficult process. It is important to maintain all of your records and communications for up to seven years while you resolve the matter in case it shows up on your credit report again.

BANKRUPTCY AND NEGATIVE INFORMATION ON CREDIT REPORTS

Identity theft is not the only life-changing event that can seriously hurt your credit score. Divorce, job loss, and medical emergencies are the most common issues that cause major damage to your financial stability and credit scores. When these challenges happen and go unsettled, they often lead to bankruptcy and foreclosure. When you are unable to pay your mortgage payments or property taxes, the lender or tax enforcement agency will file a foreclosure lawsuit against you. A foreclosure is a major negative event that will have a significant impact on your credit score. The negative impact will lessen over time. If you are able to pay other accounts as agreed, you can rebuild a solid credit score in as little as two years since this is a single trade line.

People have the tendency to think it will happen to someone else until it's them. Protect yourself by taking time to review your history. It's a good investment of your time.

A bankruptcy will have the greatest negative affect on your credit score because there are many different accounts affected on your credit report. The more accounts included in the bankruptcy, the bigger the impact will be. Like foreclosures and other derogatory items, the negative impact on your score will lessen with time.

Bankruptcies remain on your credit report for seven to ten years. All of the individual accounts within the bankruptcy should be removed from your credit report and profile within seven years of the filing date. Monitoring your credit report after a bankruptcy is critical, as accounts included in bankruptcies often do not get updated systematically.

Bankruptcy will have a major effect on various aspects of your life for years to come. It is important to do extensive research regarding your options and contact a bankruptcy attorney. In lieu of filing a bankruptcy, another option is to work with a legitimate consumer credit counseling service to get financial education, credit counseling, and debt management. These agencies contact your creditors on your behalf in an attempt to reduce the finance charges, late fees, over-limit charges, monthly payments, or time to pay off your debt.

While working with a reputable consumer credit counseling services can help, many lenders will treat this as a major negative, similar to you filing a bankruptcy.

Warning: Be careful as there are dishonest credit counseling or debt management companies that charge high fees and provide little benefit. Most of what they do can be done by the individual. Avoiding credit counseling and bankruptcy is usually the best option for you and your credit score.

Strategy: If you have the funds to pay off collections, charge offs, or judgments, negotiate a settlement with the creditor or collection agency.

Real life scenario: Frequently, when dealing with mortgage applications, we work with clients who are required to pay off collections, charge offs, tax liens, or judgments as part of their mortgage application. The most memorable example of this was a client with over $70,000 in collections and charge offs from over ten different creditors. The client had run into financial hardship due to medical issues that resulted in a failed business.

The borrower's credit score was 570 and his mortgage balance was around $145,000, which he paid perfectly. He had a stable income from a job in his field that he had been working at for over a year and a house worth $240,000. We were able to broker this loan to a national bank at 75% loan-to-value with a competitive rate. However, in order to qualify, he needed to pay off most of his collections and debt. Since his new loan was for $180,000 and we needed $150,000 to pay off his first mortgage and closing costs, we were left with $30,000 to pay off the charge offs and collections. We worked with the client and contacted all the creditors with his authorization. We negotiated settlements with all the creditors to accept around 40% of the original $70,000 balance as payment in full and closed his loan. His credit score slowly improved and he was able to refinance into a conventional mortgage two years later.

The lesson here is that in most cases, you can negotiate a settlement on your collections, charge offs, or judgments. It is common in the marketplace for your original creditor to sell this debt to a collection agency at a steep discount. The original creditor gets a tax write-off and a small amount of money. The collection agency now owns and has the right to collect the debt. They know that if they can get 50% of the original balance, they will come out ahead.

While most of the negative credit information remains on your credit report for a maximum of seven years, some information remains longer.

Public Records:

- Foreclosures remain for seven years from the date last active.
- Completed Chapter 13 bankruptcies remain for seven years from the date paid, and 10 years if not completed.
- Chapter 7, 11 and 12 bankruptcies remain for 10 years from the date filed.
- Paid tax liens remain on file for seven years from the date released (paid).
- Unpaid tax liens remain on file indefinitely.
- All judgments remain for seven years from the date filed.

Credit Accounts:

- Active accounts remain indefinitely.
- Closed accounts that were paid as agreed, typically remain for 10 years.
- Negative information remains for seven years from the date of last delinquency.

Collection and Charge Off Accounts:

- Collections and charge offs remain for seven years from the date of last delinquency.

Inquiries:

- "Hard" inquiries remain for two years. "Soft"

inquiries do not show up on your credit report.

PRIMARY LAWS THAT PROTECT CONSUMERS IN MORTGAGE TRANSACTIONS

There are many Federal laws in place to protect your rights when you apply for a mortgage. Below are some of the most important laws and protections that you should be aware of.

1. Fair Credit Reporting Act (FCRA)
2. Fair and Accurate Credit Transactions Act (FACT Act)
3. Equal Credit Opportunity Act (ECOA)
4. The Truth-in-Lending Act (TILA)

The Fair Credit Reporting Act is a Federal law that promotes the accuracy, fairness, and privacy of information in the files of consumer reporting agencies. Your major rights and protections under the FCRA are:

- You must be told if information in your file has been used against you.
- You have the right to know what is in your file.
- You have the right to ask for a credit score.
- You have the right to dispute incomplete or inaccurate information.
- Consumer reporting agencies must correct or delete inaccurate, incomplete, or unverifiable information.
- Consumer reporting agencies may not report outdated negative information.

- Access to your file is limited to those with permissible purposes.
- You must give your consent for reports to be provided to employers.
- You may limit "prescreened" offers of credit and insurance you receive based on information in your credit report.
- You may seek damages from violators.

For more information or additional rights go to www.ftc.gov/credit or write to: Federal Trade Commission, Consumer Response Center, Room 130-A, 600 Pennsylvania Ave. N.W., Washington, D.C. 20580.

The Fair and Accurate Credit Transactions Act is an amendment to the FCRA that added provisions to the law. It is designed to prevent identity theft and to allow consumers greater access to their consumer files than initially provided by the FCRA. The FACT Act also sets new standards about what can be included in a consumer report and modifies, in part, the process by which consumer disputes are handled. The major rights and protections under the FACT Act are:

- You have the right to receive a free copy of your credit report annually from each of the three credit reporting agencies. A website is maintained at www.annualcreditreport.com to request the free report.
- You have the right to place a fraud or active duty alert on your credit report.
- Credit cards, debit cards, and Social Security numbers must be truncated in specific situations.

- Financial institutions, creditors, and businesses that use credit reports must adopt a plan to detect, protect, and mitigate identity theft.
- Credit reporting agencies and any business that uses a consumer report must have policies and procedures in place to properly dispose of the sensitive documents.
- It improves accuracy and integrity of the information in credit reports and the ability to directly dispute issues with the companies that furnished it.
- It protects the privacy of consumer's medical information.
- You can opt out of marketing and information sharing among affiliated businesses.

The Equal Credit Opportunity Act (ECOA) makes it illegal for creditors to discriminate against applicants based on personal characteristics such as race, sex, age, national origin, marital status, religion, color, if you receive public assistance, or because you've exercised your rights under the Consumer Credit Protection Act.

The Consumer Credit Protection Act (CCPA) is an umbrella consumer law that includes the Equal Credit Opportunity Act, the Fair Credit Billing Act, the Fair Credit Reporting Act, and the Truth-in-Lending Act.

The Truth-in-Lending Act (TILA) requires lenders to use uniform methods for computing the cost of credit and for disclosing credit terms so consumers can simply understand how much it will cost to borrow money. TILA allows consumers to easily compare offers from multiple lenders.

Other major benefits provided by TILA are that it gives consumers the right to cancel (rescind) certain credit transactions that involve a lien (primarily a mortgage loan) on an individual's primary residence and limits your liability to $50 if your credit card is stolen, lost, or used without your authorization.

FREQUENTLY ASKED QUESTIONS ABOUT CREDIT AND CREDIT SCORES

Why is my credit score different with the three credit reporting agencies?

The three main credit reporting agencies in the United States are: Equifax, Experian, and TransUnion. Each company is independent, has different formats for collecting and storing data, and utilizes it's own proprietary algorithms in combination with FICO for scoring credit. Since they do not share credit files, if your creditor does not report to every reporting agency they won't have the same data. Additionally, when you apply for credit, the creditor may only inquire with one agency; this activity won't appear on the other two agencies.

Who is FICO and what do they do?

Fair Isaac Corporation is the company that invented the FICO® credit risk score and system. FICO scores range from 300-850, higher scores signify a stronger borrower. The system measures consumer risk and how likely they are to pay their credit obligations as agreed. Most lenders and financial institutions utilize the FICO score model available at the three major credit reporting agencies to make credit decisions.

Who is VantageScore and what do they do?

VantageScore, owned by TransUnion, is a credit score model and system that was developed by the three major credit reporting agencies. VantageScore's range from 501-990 and have familiar academic grades (A-F) associated with their model. Similar to FICO, the system measures consumer risk and how likely they are to pay their credit obligations as agreed. VantageScore is designed to score a larger population of consumers that didn't qualify for a score with FICO due to a limited credit file. Additionally, the factors that make up a VantageScore are slightly different (payment history, utilization, balances, recent credit, depth of credit, and available credit) as are percentages allocated to each factor.

If I get married, will my spouse's information and credit appear on my report?

No, credit reports are specific to each individual and do not change when you get married. If you open joint accounts like credit cards, car loans, or mortgages, these accounts will appear on both of your credit reports. One strategy to improve a new spouse's credit score if they have limited or

If you love someone enough to get married, you should know his or her credit situation as it affects you both.

poor credit is to add that person as a joint cardholder on the established spouse's credit account.

However, in the event of divorce, joint accounts can be a nightmare that could damage your credit profile. Even if the court designates your spouse to pay a specific account, your creditor will require you to pay the debt if your ex-spouse does not. Therefore, close all joint accounts and require these debts to be paid off or refinanced quickly.

Will checking your credit report hurt your credit score?

No, if you do it yourself. Personal inquiries are considered a "soft inquiry" and do not show up as an inquiry on your report or hurt your credit score. Remember, you are legally entitled to check your credit report free of charge once a year through www.annualcreditreport.com or when you get declined for a loan or credit.

What actions result in a "hard inquiry" on my credit report?

The obvious "hard inquiries" result from mortgage, credit card, or loan applications (personal, student, auto). What you might not expect is that "hard inquiries" may result from a rental application, purchasing a new cell phone, opening a new cable account, renting a car, or when requesting a credit limit increase on a credit card.

What are some negative items that could surprise you when they show up on your credit report?

You would be surprised to know various bills that go unpaid often show up on your credit report as collections and lower your score. These can include medical, gas, utility, cable, satellite, and phone (including wireless) bills. Additionally, city fines and parking tickets, buy here pay here, payday, or other personal loans, and past due child support obligations can appear. These companies or institutions may not report your payment history on a monthly basis to the credit reporting agencies. However, if you fail to pay the bills, they may file a collection against you that ultimately shows up on your credit report and affects your credit score.

While many of these items can hurt your credit, some of these accounts can help you obtain a loan when paid as agreed. If you can prove a perfect payment history, you may be able to utilize these as alternative credit references on many loan applications. This is important when you have limited credit or trade lines in your credit profile.

Can a potential employer obtain a copy of your credit report?

Yes, an employer can get a copy of your credit report if you give them permission. Your privacy is protected by the Fair Credit Reporting Act (FCRA) and restricts credit reporting agencies from providing employers, or prospective employees with your credit report without your written authorization.

What is the difference between being an authorized user on a credit card versus being a joint account holder?

An authorized user of a credit card is a person who has the right to use the card, however, they are not responsible for paying for the charges. Examples of this could be a parent who provides a credit card for their child or an employer who authorizes their accounting or operations team to use a credit card on the behalf of a business. It is recommended that the primary account holder set a low limit for these users and only add people they trust to not abuse the privilege.

Joint account holders of credit cards are both authorized to use the card and legally responsible for the balance on the account, regardless of who uses the credit card. If you agree to a joint account, make sure you receive statements and confirmation that payments are being made. If you have a joint account, you should be willing and able to make the payments in the event the other account holder is unable to do so.

In the past, people would add authorized users to their accounts in an effort to improve the credit score and history of the individual being added. However, the primary scoring models (FICO and VantageScore) caught onto this practice and currently do not consider authorized users in the calculation of scores.

Authorized user accounts, good or bad, typically show up on both parties credit reports and will be reviewed by lenders, insurers, and creditors in making underwriting decisions. If you are an authorized user and the primary cardholder doesn't make the payments, contact the creditor and be removed as an authorized user. Additionally, you will need to contact the three credit reporting agencies and dispute the trade line on your report.

What is the difference between being a joint account holder and being a co-signer for a loan or credit?

There is very little difference whether you are a joint account holder or a co-signer; you are legally responsible for the entire loan or debt that is incurred. Historically, more than half of the time, the co-signer ends up making the loan payments. Therefore, co-signing for a loan should be done with extreme caution. The negatives, financially and emotionally, usually outweigh the benefits.

Co-signing is dangerous because in most cases, the lender does not have to notify the cosigner of late payments on the account. You may not find out until you have your credit pulled or receive a call from a collection agency. At this point your credit score will have been damaged greatly.

> If someone isn't responsible with their finances, don't be certain they will be when it's yours on the line.

There is very little financial benefit to the co-signer. Even if the loan is paid on time, the debt will show up on the co-signers credit profile and could hurt their ability to get other loans in the future. Lenders rarely remove co-signers from joint accounts. The account will need to be paid in full and closed in order to separate from the primary borrower. This could be difficult if the primary borrower is having trouble making payments or doesn't qualify based on their own income, credit, and financial profile.

—3—

UNDERSTANDING THE MORTGAGE APPLICATION PROCESS

The biggest loan most of us take out in our lifetime is a mortgage. A residential mortgage loan is a loan secured against real estate on a 1-4 unit property, condo, planned unit development (PUD), townhouse, mobile, or manufactured home. Mortgage financing can be overwhelming as you have so many decisions to make. There are as many types of mortgages to choose from, just as there are many types of houses to buy, and lenders to apply with. Your goal is to obtain a mortgage with the lowest rate and fees possible in a timely and professional manner.

TRUST AND TRANSPARENCY

The best way to get a great deal on a mortgage is to be knowledgeable of the industry and marketplace. Then, work with a mortgage professional, also known as an "originator", you can trust and who is completely transparent. This person should value your business and want to maintain a long-term relationship with you. They should provide you with a low cost mortgage, competitive rates, be knowledgeable and experienced with the ability to offer multiple solutions. They need to be able to deliver on the representations they make to you and close a loan in a timely manner.

The challenge is that it is difficult to know if the mortgage professional and company you are considering has these qualities or is simply telling you what you want to hear in order to get you to apply with them. Once you sign the original application and pay for the appraisal, the representations start to fall apart.

If someone isn't transparent with you regarding their intentions, don't trust them.

Our goal is to simplify the process for you so that you can determine if the mortgage professional is trustworthy and transparent. The more you understand, the better prepared you will be when you want to purchase a new home or refinance an existing mortgage. Let's get started by answering the most common questions and decisions you need to make in the mortgage application process.

- Should you buy a home or continue to rent?
- If you buy a home, how much will you qualify for?
- What are the different steps in the loan process?
- Who decides when your credit report should be pulled or accessed?
- What is automated underwriting and how does it work?
- How does the appraisal process work?
- How long does it take to close a mortgage loan?
- What should you expect when going to your closing?
- Should you apply for a mortgage from a bank, credit union, mortgage banker, or mortgage broker?
- Should you apply for a mortgage online?
- Should you apply for a fixed or adjustable rate mortgage?
- Should you apply for a conventional, FHA, VA, USDA, jumbo, or non-conforming loan?
- Should you set up an escrow account for taxes and insurance?
- Should you lock your rate or let it float?
- Should you pay points and buy the rate down?
- What are the closing costs and how do you need to pay them?
- What documents do you need to provide to the lender?
- Why do you need to sign so many forms? Which of those forms are the most important?

Should you buy a home or continue to rent?

There are benefits and risks associated with home ownership. Deciding what is right for you will depend on your financial situation and goals. Buying may be the right move if you plan on staying in one place for a number of years, have funds for the down payment, want to build equity in real estate, and can afford the cost of repairs and maintenance on the property. As well, you will want to talk to your accountant as interest and property taxes are usually tax deductible. Pride of ownership and privacy are additional benefits to buying a home.

> Allowing yourself to be pressured into something you aren't certain of is a warning that you should wait until you are.

Renting may be ideal if you want short-term flexibility and plan on moving in the near future. Furthermore, renting is appropriate if you haven't been able to save money for the down payment required or do not have emergency funds to cover maintenance or repairs on the property when they come up.

Warning: Generally, it is not the mortgage payment that gets individuals in financial trouble when they buy a home. Instead, it is the credit card bills that result from buying new furniture, moving expenses, lawn and garden equipment, or home improvement projects. Make sure you include these costs when you decide whether or not to buy a home or continue to rent.

Assuming you decide to buy a home, let's start with the basics. Unless you pay cash when purchasing a home, you will use a mortgage loan to obtain the funds needed to close on your home and take ownership of the property. The two main legal documents are the "Note" and the "Mortgage". The Note outlines the terms of your loan, which is the loan amount, interest rate, monthly principal, and interest payments. The Note is your promise to repay the lender. In exchange, the lender provides you with the money needed to buy the home or refinance an existing loan. The mortgage is the legal document that pledges the property to the lender as security for repayment of the loan. If you stop making payments, you'll go into default and the lender can take back your property through a legal process known as foreclosure.

If you buy a home, how much will you qualify for?

Understanding what is included in your monthly mortgage payment will help you understand how much you qualify for. For underwriting purposes, your monthly payment is made up of the principal and interest on your loan, real estate taxes, and insurance (homeowners and private mortgage insurance if applicable). This is known as PITI. If you own a condo, PUD, or are part of a homeowners association, these have monthly dues that will also be included in your mortgage payment. Typically, lenders want your total PITI to be less than 30% of your monthly income. Additionally, your total debt ratio (PITI plus installment loans and revolving debt) should be less than 40%. If your overall financial and credit profile is strong, lenders may expand those ratios.

- **P**rincipal: When you repay a closed-end mortgage, a portion of the payment goes towards the principal balance. The initial principal balance is the same as your loan amount and is also known as the "amount financed".
- **I**nterest: The portion of your payment that goes to the lender to cover the cost of the loan. In the beginning of your mortgage, the majority of the payment goes towards interest and a small amount to principal.
- **T**axes: What you pay in property taxes to your county, city, or local municipality each year is divided by 12 months.
- **I**nsurance: Homeowners insurance is what you pay to protect your home against loss or damage from theft, fire, wind, natural disaster, or similar harm. The amount of homeowners insurance you pay each year is divided by 12 months.

Two other types of insurance that may be included in your monthly payment could be flood and private mortgage. Flood insurance is required if you live in a flood zone. Private Mortgage Insurance (PMI) is an insurance policy that protects the lender from the risk of you defaulting. If you obtain a mortgage at a loan-to-value greater than 80%, the lender usually requires PMI to offset the added risk.

There are two different stages in the qualifying process, pre-qualification and pre-approval. Pre-qualification is when you provide a mortgage professional with basic information like your income, assets, debts, and credit history. Based off of these representations, they will provide a preliminary estimate of what you are likely to qualify for. Typically, your financial documents have not been provided and your credit has not been reviewed. This is a great place to start when you are beginning to shop for a home and mortgage. Lenders or brokers are able to inform you what the current market rates are and give you an idea of what your monthly principal and interest payment could be. Once you are committed to buying a home and determine which mortgage professional will provide you with the best combination of service, rates, and fees, then move to the pre-approval stage.

Pre-approval is the process of completing a mortgage application and submitting your financial documents to your originator. They will review your paperwork and pull your credit. If needed, they will submit your file through an automated underwriting decision engine. Once this process is completed, you will receive a pre-approval letter from the lender or broker. This is important because it tells realtors and sellers that you are serious about buying a home and states the price range that you qualify for. Without a pre-approval letter, your offer may not be taken seriously.

What are the different steps in the loan process?

While each mortgage application is unique, the typical steps you will go through from application to closing a mortgage are outlined below:

Step 1 – General inquiry and pre-qualification: As mentioned earlier, pre-qualification is when you provide an originator with basic information like your income, assets, debts, and credit history. Based off of these representations, they will provide a preliminary estimate of what you are likely to qualify for on a purchase or if there will be a benefit to you to refinance your current mortgage. The originator may pull your credit during this stage or wait until you want to move forward with the application.

Step 2 – Initial application and disclosures: The initial application and disclosures are the beginning to the loan process. After you have signed a purchase contract or decided you want to proceed with a refinance, you will complete a mortgage application (Form 1003) with your originator. Within three business days of completing the application, you are required to receive a copy of the application to sign (you should

Never sign any blank documents that will be filled in later. Be aware of your responsibilities before you sign anything.

update any information that is missing or incorrect) along with a Good Faith Estimate (GFE) and Truth-in-Lending (TIL) statement which itemizes the rate, costs, and finance charges associated with obtaining the loan. There will be additional disclosures provided to you to sign, however, the above are the most important documents. You will return the signed application and disclosures along with the supporting documents (income, assets, etc.) needed to process your loan file to your originator.

Step 3 – Processing and automated underwriting: Processing a mortgage file involves the originating mortgage company, reviewing your application, and supporting documentation. The person completing these duties is known as a processor. This includes verifying the information on the application against your credit report, income documents, purchase contract (if applicable), asset statements, and other applicable documents. Once your application has been updated and verified, the processor will submit your file through the appropriate automated underwriting platform to get an approval. When approval is received, the processor will order the appraisal, additional verifications, title work, and payoffs. Upon receipt of your appraisal, the processor will put together the entire package and submit it to their underwriting department. If you are working with a mortgage broker, they will submit your loan file to a lender's underwriting department.

Step 4 – Underwriting: Underwriting is the process of assessing the risk of offering a mortgage to a borrower. The underwriter will focus on the three C's (credit, collateral, and capacity) of mortgage underwriting when reviewing the loan file. Underwriters validate the accuracy of the borrower's application, documentation, and findings from the automated underwriting computer models and apply them to the lender and secondary market guidelines for approving the mortgage.

How long your loan is in underwriting is usually based on the volume of business and infrastructure of the lender. Additionally, the quality and completeness of the loan file aids in determining how long the process will take. Once the underwriter reviews the loan file, they will issue a conditional approval or suspend the loan file until they acquire the required information to make a decision. The conditional approval outlines the additional requirements needed before final approval is granted. The processor is in charge of obtaining the additional documentation from the borrower or third party and sending them to the underwriting for final review. When all conditions are satisfied, the underwriter will issue a clear to close to the processor and originator.

Step 5 – Closing: Closing or settlement is the process whereby you sign the final legal paperwork and the title to the property is transferred to the buyer on a purchase. Lastly, the mortgage (or "deed of trust" as it is called in certain states) is given to the lender by the buyer/borrower, and the funds are collected and disbursed.

Mortgage closings are completed through a settlement agent, which is usually a title company, escrow company, or attorney. The settlement agent will do the following:

- Search and examine public records related to you and the subject property's title.
- Obtain the payoffs.
- Ensure the liens are paid off.
- Prepare the HUD-1 settlement statement and closing documents according to the lenders instructions.
- Explain and notarize the closing documents to the borrower and seller. Issue a title insurance policy to the buyer and lender.
- Hold deposits and disburse the funds for the transaction to all the parties involved.

- Record the legal documents necessary to complete the purchase or refinance.

Who decides when your credit report should be accessed?

This is a decision that you will make. The mortgage applicant must authorize the originator to pull your credit. Be careful of working with individuals or companies who want to access your credit file without explaining the mortgage process, providing you with basic information, and answering your questions.

> When it comes to decisions that will affect you, everyone may not care so don't give your power away.

In most instances, experienced mortgage professionals can ask you appropriate questions without reviewing your credit report and provide you with a valid quote. Inexperienced loan originators often want to pull your credit, review your file with a manager, and then get back to you with a quote.

When your file is underwritten, the lender will usually require a current (within 30 days) tri-merged credit report from an approved credit provider. A tri-merged report includes the credit file and credit score from Equifax, TransUnion, and Experian. The middle credit score of the borrower(s) is typically utilized to meet underwriting guidelines and for pricing on the loan. This report must come directly from the originating banker, broker, or lender. Neither the borrower nor another party can provide the report. This is why every company you complete an application with for a mortgage may pull your credit report.

Real life scenario: You are looking to refinance your current 30-year fixed rate mortgage to a 15-year fixed rate mortgage. You inform the originator that you've never missed a payment in your life, you have very little credit card debt, and you owe $200,000 on a home that is worth approximately $350,000. Furthermore, you have a stable income of $120,000 a year, significant liquid assets, and your credit score was 765 when you purchased a new car three months ago.

In this scenario, you don't need to have your credit pulled by the originator to provide you with a quote. They should know you are going to qualify for a conventional mortgage. They can share what the market rates and fees are, as well as review the benefits of the refinance loan with you without pulling your credit.

Warning: When your credit is pulled in connection with a mortgage application, expect to get solicited heavily by mortgage companies through direct mail and telemarketing. The credit reporting agencies sell your information, which is known in the mortgage industry as "trigger data". The justification is that competition from mortgage companies will lead to better terms for you. However, the reality is that the companies who purchase the trigger data usually employ inexperienced mortgage originators and have aggressive sales strategies to get you to work with their company.

What is automated underwriting and how does it work?

Automated underwriting are systems and technology platforms created by the two largest companies that purchase and sell mortgages in the secondary market, Fannie Mae and Freddie Mac. This technology allows computer models to assess the risk of default based on many factors within the current loan file against historical data from hundreds of thousands of mortgages.

Originators use these systems on the front end of the loan transaction to obtain conditional approvals and then the lender's underwriter will validate the findings when they underwrite the loan file. Automated underwriting has streamlined the mortgage process by providing analysis of the income, credit, assets, and loan terms in minutes rather than days. Furthermore, these systems have reduced the amount of documentation the borrower needs to provide to the lender. The system will tailor the amount of documentation needed in proportion to the risk on the loan file.

How does the appraisal process work?

Your property value is a critical piece of the mortgage underwriting process. The appraisal process is a comprehensive review of the property and market conditions in order to assign a value to the real property. The loan type, loan purpose, automated underwriting approval, and lender requirements will dictate the type of appraisal required. Your originator or their processor will order the appraisal from a licensed appraisal or appraisal management company as required for the transaction.

The appraisal typically costs between $300 and $500 and is usually paid by you directly to the appraiser or appraisal management company prior to service being completed. The cost will vary based on the report required, property type, location, square footage, and appraiser or appraisal management company used. Investment properties, multi-unit properties, and properties in rural areas will usually cost more than a single-family residence in a heavily populated area. The most common type of appraisal is the Uniform Residential Appraisal Report (URAR). This report consists of interior and exterior photos, comparable sales, and a complete cost breakdown of the property.

Make sure you know your realistic value.

The lender will use the appraised value to determine what the maximum loan amount is that they will offer to you. For purchases, the lender will use the lower of the appraised value or purchase price to determine the maximum loan amount. Additionally, the lender will thoroughly review the value and completeness of the appraisal in the underwriting process. This review may come from a neutral third party appraiser, a broker-price opinion, or through an Automated Valuation Model (AVM), which is a technology platform that will come up with a value for the property. Lenders typically will allow for a variance of 10%, however, anything above this will be questioned significantly and may cause your loan to be suspended or declined.

If you want to research real estate properties values on your own, there are several real estate websites that provide online estimates within seconds. While these websites provide a lot of useful information such as transaction history for the subject property and recent sales nearby the property, a lender will not accept their value estimates.

Warning: Make sure you are confident in and committed to working with the originator prior to paying for the appraisal. Many times, the appraisal is not transferable to a new originator or lender. If you want to go with a different offer, you will end up paying for a second appraisal.

It is important for you to know that you have the right to promptly review any appraisal, computer valuation, appraisal review, or other data pertaining to your

Be apprised of your rights to avoid things going wrong.

property's value that is used during the loan process. This rule is intended to give you the time and opportunity to challenge any errors in the reports. You can ask any questions or address any errors with your mortgage professional, real estate agent, or other financial advisor as soon as possible. Do not wait until closing when it may be too late to make any changes.

How long does it take to close a mortgage loan?

The industry standard for closing a mortgage from initial application to funding the loan is 25-45 days. However, there are many variables that can allow for the loan to close quicker or take longer. The main factors that affect the timetable include the type of loan applied for, property type, whether or not you have provided a complete application and all of the required documentation. Other determining factors are the capabilities of the mortgage originator and their support staff, the quality and competence of the third party providers (appraisal and title), in addition to the lenders underwriting proficiency and infrastructure.

What should you expect when going to closing?

The closing process for a mortgage loan can be a stressful process or a simple formality depending on how professionally your loan transaction has been handled. You should ask to review the final loan application and HUD-1 (closing statement that explains the financial transaction) prior to going to closing. Lenders and brokers are legally required to provide the borrower a copy of the HUD-1 one day prior to closing. If there are any inconsistencies, it is better to address them immediately with your originator versus waiting to do so at closing.

Closings are customarily coordinated through an attorney, escrow, or title company. In addition to providing closing services, these companies provide various services for the loan transaction. The primary services include a lien search on the property and borrower, a property search, receive and disburse funds from and to all parties associated with the transaction, provide a title insurance policy for the borrower and lender, and record the mortgage with the proper county.

Closing a purchase loan is a little more complicated as there are many more parties involved. However, the main difference between closing a purchase versus refinancing a primary residence is when the funds are disbursed. For all purchase loans and refinances on non-owner occupied or second homes, the loan is funded the same business day. For owner-occupied refinances, the loan is funded after the three-business day rescission period has expired.

If it doesn't feel right, exercise your right to reconsider. It's better than going through with something you may regret.

The right of rescission is the borrower's legal right to cancel the refinance loan within three business days from the closing date. When you exercise your right to rescind the loan, you completely cancel the transaction and everything remains in place as it was prior to the closing. Your new lender will not fund your loan until the rescission period has expired. However, once it has expired, the lender wires money to the attorney, escrow, or title company. They are responsible for paying off any liens on the property, along with any other debts instructed by the lender, and disbursing funds to the appropriate parties associated with the transaction.

Should you get a mortgage from a bank, credit union, mortgage banker, or mortgage broker?

There are advantages and disadvantages with each business or financial institution. Generally speaking, brokers are able to obtain the lowest rates in the marketplace; however, their fees are typically the highest. Brokers have multiple loan programs and numerous lenders they work with. Professional service and the ability to close loans quickly are completely based on which broker you work with. Banks and credit unions tend to have the lowest fee, but their rates are traditionally a little higher. Additionally, banks and credit unions don't have as many loan programs available and it usually takes longer to close your loan. Mortgage bankers tend to fall in the middle. Their rates, fees, and loan programs are similar to that of a broker. Successful mortgage bankers tend to have the best combination of professional service and the ability to close your loan quickly.

The type of company that originates your loan is less important than the rate you receive, fees you pay, experience of your mortgage advisor, and the ability to close your loan in a professional and timely manner. If you qualify for a conventional loan with a broker or banker you will qualify for a conventional loan with a bank or credit union because most loans are underwritten to the same guidelines regardless of origination source. The challenge is that there are so many different loan programs and the underwriting guidelines can change. Working with an experienced mortgage professional can make a big difference, especially when it comes to self-employed borrowers, unique properties, or borrowers with less than perfect credit or small down payments.

The challenge is that it is hard to know these facts if you haven't worked with the company or individual previously. Speaking with different individuals and comparing multiple offers can help you make a better decision. Additionally, mortgage professionals are required to be licensed or registered through the Nationwide Mortgage Licensing System. Go to the following website www.nmlsconsumeraccess.org to find out more about the company or individual you are contemplating working with.

Since the financial crisis in 2007 and 2008, the regulatory community has completely changed the landscape of mortgage origination. In addition to the licensing or registration of mortgage originators, there are limits on the fees borrowers can be charged, loan types are limited, and tougher underwriting requirements make it more difficult to qualify for a loan. Many of these changes were necessary to protect borrowers and the economy from another housing bust. Other times, the changes were political, caused delays to the process, and additional costs to the borrower.

Should you apply for a mortgage online?

The Internet is a great place to research information when considering a major purchase or financial transaction. There is nothing wrong with applying for a mortgage online, just know the facts and understand the risks. When you apply, most times it will be with a marketing company that resells your loan information to multiple originators or other marketing

Take time to check someone's credentials, as it will add another layer of protection and comfort to your process.

companies. This competition may lead to lower rates and fees; however, your patience may get tested as you receive multiple solicitations. More importantly, only apply with companies that don't require your Social Security number. You don't want identity theft to occur.

Another thing you should know is that the advertised rate is not always the market rate. In order to get your attention or application, the rates advertised often require you to pay multiple points or accept an adjustable rate mortgage. Rarely is it in your best interest to pay points to buy the rate down.

The best place to start is with a mortgage professional who did an excellent job for you in the past. If you don't have one or remember who that is, ask for a referral from a trusted individual, financial professional, or realtor. If you are looking to refinance your current mortgage, contacting the lender who you make the payments to is another option.

You don't always have to look for a mortgage professional, they will find you. Besides purchasing Internet leads from the online marketing companies, mortgage companies typically use telemarketing, direct mail, trigger data, social media, radio, or television advertising to reach you.

Should you set up an escrow account for taxes and insurance?

When you make your monthly payment, where does the money go? The principal and interest goes to the lender. The principal is applied to your loan balance while the interest is income to the lender. If your payment includes property taxes and homeowners insurance, this amount is deposited into an escrow account held by the lender. If you have flood insurance or Homeowners Association dues, the lender will deposit these into the escrow account. If you have mortgage insurance, that amount will be paid to the third party insurance company providing the insurance.

With most lenders, when the loan-to-value is at or below 80%, then it is the borrowers choice if they want to set up an escrow account. If the borrower prefers to pay the taxes and homeowners insurance directly, they can "waive escrows" and the monthly mortgage payment will be their principal and interest. Some lenders charge a fee or increase your rate slightly if you waive escrows. Setting up an escrow account will not affect whether or not you get approved for a mortgage.

Lenders usually require escrow accounts on loans with a loan-to-value greater than 80% due to the added risk for high loan-to-value mortgages, the lender wants to make sure the taxes and insurance are paid. Having an escrow account can be convenient and beneficial, especially for those who don't have significant savings. For some, adding an equal amount each month to their mortgage payment is easier than paying a large semi-annual or annual bill. When the tax or insurance bill comes due, the lender will pay it directly.

When you have an escrow account, your monthly mortgage payment may change. By law, lenders may not keep more then two months of reserves in your account; therefore, they complete an analysis of your escrow account each year. Often, this results in your monthly payment changing because your property taxes or homeowners insurance has changed. If you have a fixed-rate mortgage, the principal and interest portion of the mortgage payment will never change.

Warning: When you build or purchase a newly constructed home, the property tax bill is usually based on the assessed value for the raw land that your home is now built on. Because lenders are only allowed to keep up to two months of reserves in your escrow account, they base your monthly payment on the current property tax bill. Once the county auditor assesses the properties value (house and land), there will be a new tax bill associated with the real estate. You should be prepared for a significant increase in your monthly payment, the more expensive the home, the larger the bill. Make sure to ask the realtor, builder, title company, or mortgage professional what the projected taxes will be so that you can effectively plan. Failing to pay your property taxes will result in the county filing a foreclosure against your property. This is another reason why lenders prefer to set up escrow accounts for borrowers.

Should you apply for a fixed or adjustable-rate mortgage?

One of the first decisions you will make is whether you want a fixed or adjustable-rate mortgage (ARM). With a fixed-rate mortgage your interest rate along with your principal and interest payment remain the same for the life of the loan. Terms for fixed rates range from ten to forty years, with fifteen and thirty-year terms being the most popular. An adjustable-rate mortgage is subject to change either on specific dates or based on market conditions. Payments for an adjustable-rate mortgage are usually fixed for a number of years that range from one to ten, with three and five being the most common. Adjustable-rate loans usually have a payment and amortization schedule based on a thirty-year term.

Taking what you are offered may not be what you need. Arm yourself with proper knowledge about the process to avoid being taken advantage of.

When deciding between a fixed and adjustable-rate the choice is based on your goals and plans. Fixed rates are great because they provide security and stability in knowing that your payment won't change. Fixed rates are ideal in low-rate environments or when you plan on staying in the home for a long period of time. Adjustable rates are great if you want a lower monthly payment, plan on being in a home for a short period of time, or in a high-rate environment. Historically, thirty-year fixed-rate mortgages are between .5% and 1% higher than fifteen-year fixed mortgages. Depending on the fixed period of an adjustable rate mortgage, historically the rate is between .5% and 1.5% less than a thirty-year fixed.

Real life scenario: Five years ago, you purchased your home for $150,000 and took out a thirty-year fixed mortgage at 5.5% at $135,000 with a $766.52 principal and interest payment. Because you only put 10% down, you were required to have mortgage insurance that cost $58.50 per month. Mortgage rates have been dropping and you look into refinancing. Your mortgage payoff is $126,000 and home appraised for $170,000. The new loan is for $130,000, which will cover paying off your existing mortgage, setting up a new escrow account and prepaid interest (estimated to be $2,000), in addition to the closing costs (estimated to be $2,000). Your credit is excellent and your income is stable. You qualify for every mortgage. The question is, which mortgage are you going to choose? Let's look at the four most popular loan types with theoretical rates:

Loan Options

Option	Loan Type & Rate	Payment	Monthly Savings
1	30-year fixed at 4.5%	$658.69	$107.83
2	15-year fixed at 3.5%	$929.35	$162.83 (Monthly Increase)
3	5/1 ARM at 3.5%	$583.76	$182.76
4	3/1 ARM at 3.25%	$565.77	$200.75

The first factor to consider is how long you plan on staying in the home. If you are moving within the next twelve months, you should not refinance your mortgage, as the benefits associated with the new loan will not offset the costs. If you are planning on moving in the next three to four years, a 5/1 ARM will provide you with better monthly savings compared to a 30-year fixed loan, while maintaining a fixed-rate for the first five years. If you are planning on staying in the home for a long time and you can comfortably afford the payments, the 15-year fixed is the best choice for you. If your budget is tight, you lack an emergency fund, or if you are unsure how long you plan on living in the home, the 30-year fixed loan would be the best for you.

Once you choose the ideal loan type for your financial situation, review the monthly payment or long-term interest savings against the costs associated with the new loan. An added benefit received from refinancing is that the mortgage insurance premium will go away as your new loan is less then 80% loan-to-value. Therefore, depending on the loan type chosen, your monthly savings will be between $166 and $259 a month. If you chose to go with the 15-year mortgage, your payment would increase $104 a month. However, the total of your payments will be $167,283, if you pay the loan as agreed until paid off. Compare that to your previous 30-year fixed loan. You have twenty-five years left to pay $766.52, but if you don't refinance and pay that loan, you will pay $229,956 in principal and interest until paid off. Going with a 15-year mortgage will save you $62,673 in interest. This is why we recommend borrowing for the shortest term that is affordable.

There are other factors to consider when choosing between a fixed and adjustable rate mortgage. These include your job security or opportunities, current savings or emergency fund, other debt you have, future loans you plan on applying for, current credit scores and profile, or the likelihood of refinancing the mortgage in the future. Other times, structuring your loan properly to receive an underwriting approval will determine whether you obtain a fixed or adjustable-rate mortgage. Working with an experienced and ethical mortgage professional can help you understand your options and recommend a solution that is ideal for you.

Should you apply for a conventional, FHA, VA, USDA, jumbo, or non-conforming loan?

The next big decision you need to make is which loan program is best for you. The different loan programs are conventional, Federal Housing Administration (FHA), Department of Veterans Affairs (VA), United States Department of Agriculture (USDA), and non-conforming. Each loan program has its own set of underwriting guidelines and loan limits. Working with an experienced mortgage professional can help you compare options and decide which program is best for you.

What determines which program is best for you depends on your credit score and profile, the loan-to-value (down payment on a purchase), and your income (stability and debt-to-income ratio). Additionally, the property type, occupancy status, your personal assets, and current mortgage type (refinance) will play a significant role in the mortgage program that you qualify for and is ideal for your situation.

Conventional (conforming) mortgages adhere to the loan limits and underwriting guidelines set forth by Fannie Mae and Freddie Mac, the Government Sponsored Enterprises (GSE's). The GSE's do not originate mortgage loans; they buy them from lenders and sell them in the secondary market. A conventional loan is not insured or guaranteed by the Federal Government. Conventional loans are ideal for borrowers with excellent credit and a considerable down payment or equity in their home. Conventional loans can be used to finance an owner-occupied, second home, or investment property. While conventional loans are more conservative then other loan programs, they tend to have the best rates and terms for the borrower.

An FHA loan is a mortgage that is insured by the Federal Housing Administration. Individuals with less than perfect credit or low down payments usually elect FHA loans. These loans are owner-occupied only and the rates are comparable to conventional mortgages. The biggest difference is the mortgage insurance premiums that are required for FHA loans. Essentially the federal government charges an upfront insurance premium and a monthly premium to offset the risk of loss in case the borrower defaults. The FHA recalculates the loan limits each year. In low cost areas, the loan limit can be as low as 65% of the conforming loan limit. In high cost areas, the loan limit can be a maximum of 150% of the conforming loan limit. For example, the conforming loan limit in 2015 remains at $417,000. Therefore, in low cost areas, the FHA loan limit will remain at $271,050 (65% of $417,000). Meanwhile, in high cost areas, the FHA loan limit will remain at the national ceiling of $625,000 (150% of $417,000). The FHA loan limit in most counties is less than the conforming loan limit.

A VA loan is a mortgage that is guaranteed by the Department of Veterans Affairs. VA loans are owner-occupied and exclusively for individuals who have served or are presently serving in the U.S. military. The benefits to VA mortgages are: they do not require down payments, the credit scores and profiles are similar to FHA, meaning they are not as strict as conventional, interest rates are comparable to FHA and conventional loans. While VA loans do not charge mortgage insurance, there is a "funding fee" charged.

The United States Department of Agriculture (USDA) helps low-to-moderate income individuals in rural areas buy, refinance, or renovate a home. There are no down payment requirements, flexible credit guidelines, and competitive rates. USDA loans are only offered as 30-year fixed mortgages. There is a Guaranty Fee required; however, it can be financed into the loan.

A jumbo mortgage is a loan that is larger than the conventional loan limits as established by the GSE's. Currently, the maximum loan amount you can obtain for a conventional loan on a single-family residence is $417,000. Jumbo loans require borrowers to have similar credit and asset profiles as conventional borrowers. The rates are usually .25%-.50% higher than conventional loans.

Non-conforming loans are those loans that do not meet the underwriting guidelines of Fannie Mae or Freddie Mac (GSE's) and are not insured or guaranteed by the Federal Government. Non-conforming loans usually incur higher rates and fees to offset the additional risk. Jumbo mortgages are considered non-conforming because of their loan size.

Should you lock your rate or let it float?

The textbook answer is in a rising rate environment, you should lock your loan. In a stable or falling rate environment, you should float the rate and lock days prior to closing. The problem is that it is impossible to predict what the rates are going to do from day-to-day. Mortgage rates fluctuate like the stock market. In fact, rates are closely tied to the yield on the 10-year Treasury index.

There are many variables that will determine how quickly your loan will close. The first factor is how timely you can return the initial application, disclosures, and financial documents to the originator. Other factors depend upon how competent the loan originator and processor are, whether the loan is a purchase or a refinance, what loan program you are applying for, how busy the underwriting department is, and what type of property is being financed. On average, it takes between 25 and 45 days to close most mortgage applications. If you are conservative or concerned rates are going up, you can lock your rate early in the process. However, you will have to lock for a longer period of time. The longer lock period may result in a slightly higher rate, assuming that rates were stable.

Find out early in the process what the lenders policy is on locking rates. Most likely, you will not be able to lock until you have a completed application and submitted your financial paperwork. Other lenders require a completed appraisal or final underwriting approval before you are able to lock your interest rate. Locking a rate is a commitment from you to your lender or broker.

Should you pay points and buy the rate down?

Under most circumstances, we would not recommend it as you are adding fees to your loan. Discount points are effectively prepaid interest and used to buy your rate down. One point is equal to one percent of the loan amount. For example, on a $200,000 loan, one point equals $2,000. Paying one point usually reduces your rate by .25% and takes between five and six years to break even. If you sell the property or refinance before the breakeven point, you will not offset the cost associated with points.

There are times when paying points to buy the rate down does make sense. These include when you qualify for a loan as a result of the lower rate and payment or when the seller has agreed to pay points as an incentive to purchase their property.

Warning: There are builders that offer buyers below market financing if you agree to obtain a loan from their affiliated mortgage company. Effectively what the builder does is raise the price of the home by thousands of dollars to cover the cost of buying the rate down. This may give you a lower monthly payment. However, the added cost to your home could cause you problems if you try to sell or refinance your home in the near future. This goes against one of the basic rules, borrow the least amount possible. We recommend negotiating a lower purchase price for the home and taking a market interest rate.

What are closing costs and how do you need to pay them?

Your originator is required by law to provide you with a Good Faith Estimate (GFE) of the closing costs associated with your loan within three business days of you making an application. Closing fees, also called settlement costs, cover almost every expense associated with your home loan. These fees vary by state, mortgage type, and lender. Nevertheless, between $2,200 and $3,000 is the national average. The main fees involved are origination, application, credit report, processing, underwriting, appraisal, closing, title search and title insurance.

Government loan programs with upfront mortgage insurance, funding, or Guaranty Fees will increase the total closing costs, however these fees are usually financed into the loan. The GFE in conjunction with the Truth-in-Lending (TIL) disclosure is meant to allow you to review the closing costs and effectively shop for a mortgage between multiple originators.

Warning: Do not pay upfront application fees, the mortgage marketplace is extremely competitive and most lenders or brokers do not charge application fees. The only fees you should pay prior to closing are for the appraisal and credit report. The remainder of the fees will be paid through the closing of the loan. When you purchase a home, you can often negotiate for the seller to pay some or all of your closing costs. When you refinance a loan, these may be included in the new loan, however you can bring money to closing to pay them if you want.

Real life scenario: How can an originator offer a no-closing cost refinance? It is simple, they increase the mortgage rate and use added revenue received from the investor/lender for selling a higher rate to pay your closing costs. This can be an effective strategy, especially if you plan on moving or refinancing again within the next five years as your loan balance is usually less. When you are shopping for a loan, review your options and decide which is better for you. Below is a realistic comparison.

No Closing Cost Comparison

Closing Costs:	Standard $3,000	No closing cost option
Mortgage Amount:	$203,000	$200,000
Interest Rate:	4.25%	5.00%
Term:	360 months	360 months
Type:	30-year fixed	30-year fixed
Program:	Conventional	Conventional
P&I Payment:	$998.64	$1,073.64

As you can see in the above example, the monthly payment is $75 less by paying the standard closing costs. On the other hand, your principal amount owed started $3,000 higher. Deciding which way to go really depends on the closing costs, difference in rates, how long you plan on staying in the home, the opportunity to refinance in the future, and the underwriting guidelines.

What documents do you need to provide to the lender?

Lenders want to know that you are a low risk for default and have the ability to repay the loan. This is accomplished by verifying your income, credit, assets, and other financial information. Some of the documents that you should have ready when you start the process are:

1. Last two years of income. This will include the last two years of your Federal tax returns, W-2's, 1099's. If you are self-employed, you

should have your last two years of business tax returns readily available.

2. Last 30 days of income. This will include your last two paystubs. If you are self-employed, this will be a recent profit and loss statement. If you receive other income, compile your last three months of bank statements.

3. Other income such as Social Security, pension, child support, alimony, worker's compensation, disability, VA or retirement benefits, or other income, require the award letter or legal paperwork outlining the income and benefit. Most underwriting guidelines require that the income will continue for three or more years to be able to be included on your application.

4. Asset statements. This includes your last three months bank statements along with your last two investment and retirement statements.

5. Proof of mortgage or rent payments. If your mortgage is on your credit report, this will be sufficient. Otherwise, the lender may ask for copies of your last twelve months of cancelled checks for your mortgage or rent.

6. Insurance agent's name and contact information. A copy of your current declaration's page for your homeowner's policy if you own the home that is being refinanced.

7. When purchasing a home, you will need to provide the purchase contract and addendums along with proof of any earnest money deposit.

8. If you are refinancing, provide a copy of the previous HUD-1 settlement statement and

Note. The HUD-1 is the legal document required at closing that itemizes the services and fees charged to the borrower, the parties involved in the transaction, and outlines the financial transaction and final numbers.

9. Prepare a list of creditors and recent statements. Include credit cards, student loans, mortgage statements, or auto statements.
10. You will need a copy of your divorce decree, if applicable.
11. Provide a copy of your bankruptcy paperwork, if applicable.

The lender may not require all of these documents, yet having them readily available will speed up the process. The better your credit and profile, the less documentation you will need. Additionally, fully disclosing everything in the application process will eliminate surprises that could cause your loan to be declined.

Warning: Two of the most overlooked items in the pre-approval process are child support income or expenses and 401(k) loans, as they don't show up on your credit report. If these are not taken into consideration, the amount you qualify for will not be correct. While an inexperienced loan originator may disregard these issues in the pre-approval process, the underwriter will not. There is nothing more frustrating than going through the entire loan process, paying for an appraisal, and then getting declined.

Why do you need to sign so many forms? Which of those forms are the most important?

There is no way around it, you will have to sign a multitude of paperwork when you initially apply for a mortgage and then again when you go to closing. The application and disclosures are required by Federal and state laws and meant to educate and protect you, the borrower.

Don't sign something that you have not read thoroughly or don't understand. The little things people skim over or don't question are what can cause damage later.

While you should read all the documents, the primary documents you need to pay attention to when applying for a mortgage are the application (typically called the 1003), the Good Faith Estimate (GFE), and the Truth-in-Lending (TIL). The application provides you and the lender with the type of mortgage applied for, the terms of the loan, the property information, purpose of the loan, personal information, employment information, monthly income, housing expenses, assets, liabilities, details of the transactions, personal declarations, signatures, and final information. The GFE is a written estimate of all the closing fees, prepaid charges, and escrow items that are expected to complete your mortgage loan. The TIL provides information about the cost of your credit allowing you to review multiple offers by comparing the Annual Percentage Rate (APR). The TIL will include the APR, the finance charge, the amount financed, the total payments made, and include the proposed monthly payment schedule. The application, GFE, and TIL are required to be delivered to the borrower within three business days of making an application with the originator.

When you go to closing, you will have to resign many of the same documents that were originally signed at application. You will want to review the 1003, GFE, and TIL and make sure major changes have not been made. Government regulations do not allow lenders or brokers to increase the rate or fees to a borrower without a valid reason. In addition, they must fully disclose the change in circumstance to the borrower(s) prior to closing. The most important documents at closing will be the HUD-1 settlement statement, the Mortgage, and the Note. The HUD-1 itemizes the services and fees charged to the borrower, the parties involved in the transaction (borrower, property details, settlement agent, lender, and seller if a purchase), and outlines the financial transaction and final numbers. The Mortgage is the legal document that pledges the property to the lender as security for providing the funds to you. The Note outlines the terms of your loan, loan amount, interest rate, and monthly principal and interest payments. The Note is your promise to repay the lender in exchange the lender provides you with the money needed to buy the home or refinance an existing loan.

What caused the housing market to crash in 2007 and 2008?

The answer is simple, greed. Everyone involved was making or receiving a significant amount of money. It started in the late 1990's and didn't stop until property values started to fall in 2007. The major dysfunctions in the banking system came from poor underwriting standards, unethical business practices, and creative loan programs:

1. Borrowers with limited to poor credit were approved for mortgages with little or no money down.
2. Individuals with little or no income, disclosed on the application, were approved for loans. No Income, No Job, No Assets were known as the famous NINJA loans.
3. Properties were being appraised at unrealistic values and major repairs were overlooked.
4. Interest only and negative amortization loans were aggressively being marketed and sold. These creative loan programs allowed borrowers to have artificially low payments and the deferred amount was added to the principal balance on the loan.
5. Real estate was being bought and sold, "flipped" in a short period of time, sometimes the same day. Many times improvements had not been made to the property, yet it would be resold to borrowers for tens of thousands of dollars more than the property was just purchased for and really worth.
6. Borrowers were being charged high rates and fees for mortgages.

Few parties paid attention to the problems that were developing in the real estate market until it was too late. The economy was doing well, which led to the rise in mortgage interest rates and a slow down in the housing market. Eventually, the wild increases in property values reversed course and the bubble burst in 2007.

To pass the blame on one group or reason for the housing bust is totally misrepresenting how everyone was involved. While not every individual or company acted with greed or total disregard to basic lending and real estate fundamentals, it was easy to look the other way because there was so much money being made.

—4—

UNDERSTANDING UNDERWRITING STANDARDS

One of the challenges in the mortgage market is that underwriting guidelines can change with little notice. Prior to the housing crash of 2007 and 2008, the underwriting standards were extremely relaxed and getting approved for a mortgage was easy. After the crash, underwriting procedures became rigorous making it difficult to get approved for a new loan, especially for self-employed borrowers and individuals with less than perfect credit or little assets.

Regulation has made it costly for lenders to take on additional risk. If they do, lenders are often required to repurchase the loan if it goes into default or face legal and regulatory fines and penalties. Underwriting standards will loosen as property values increase and the risk of loss to the lenders is reduced. We are starting to see additional loan programs coming to the marketplace, especially for the self-employed borrower who has excellent credit and assets, even when their tax return income isn't great.

Underwriting guidelines are different depending on the mortgage or property type you choose. However, the fundamentals for underwriting residential mortgages focus on the three C's (credit, collateral, and capacity).

- **Credit:** What is your credit score and how have you paid your obligations in the past? Your mortgage history is the most important.
- **Collateral:** What is the condition of the property, what type of property is securing the loan, and will you be living in the home? An owner-occupied property is less risky than an investment property.
- **Capacity:** Do you have the ability to make the mortgage payments? Specifically, what is your monthly income and resulting debt-to-income ratio? Furthermore, the underwriter will consider your savings and other liquid financial assets you have, known as reserves.

In addition to having a good understanding of the application process, it is a good idea to have a basic knowledge of the main underwriting guidelines for the different mortgage loans. When you understand the rules, you can effectively take actions that will help you obtain a loan with the best rates and terms. Below are some of the important questions we hope you will understand by the end of this chapter.

- What are the credit score requirements?
- What are reserves and why are they important?
- What is the down payment required to get a mortgage loan?
- What is Private Mortgage Insurance (PMI) and how does it affect a borrower?
- What is Loan-to-Value (LTV) and why is it important?
- What is debt-to-income ratio (DR) and why is it important?
- Why does it matter what type of property you own or purchase?
- How does being self-employed affect my ability to get a mortgage?
- What is the difference between an owner-occupied, second home, and investment property?

What are the credit score requirements?

Your credit score and profile are critical when you apply for a mortgage. The higher your score, the more programs you will qualify for and the lower the rates will be.

FICO scores are used by most underwriting decision models and credit repositories in the mortgage industry. FICO scores range between 300 and 850, with the average score in America around 695. The following is a good reference on how scores are judged.

FICO Credit Score Chart

Score	Grading
720+	Excellent Credit
660-719	Good Credit
620-659	Fair Credit
580-619	Marginal Credit
Below 579	Poor Credit

Conventional and jumbo mortgage loans have the highest credit score requirements. They are intended for borrowers with excellent credit. Many borrowers in the good credit category qualify for conventional or jumbo loans. However, those with fair or worse credit will have difficulty getting approved.

Government loans, FHA, VA, and USDA are more lenient with the credit scores for borrowers. Loans are often approved for borrowers with fair credit or better. Occasionally, borrowers within the marginal or poor credit category can get approved.

Previous to the housing crisis, borrowers with poor and bad credit were likely to get a loan. Today, there are extremely limited choices. On occasion, borrowers are able to get approved through "hard money" lenders. However, these lenders charge higher interest rates and fees to offset the additional risk.

What are reserves and why are they important?

Reserves are funds (liquid assets) you have available after closing your loan. This includes your checking and savings accounts, investments, and retirement accounts. Reserves are especially important because the more assets you have, the less likely you are to default on your mortgage. In case of an emergency, such as you lose your job or have a major medical incident, you are more likely to weather the challenge and continue to make your mortgage payment because you have money saved.

Conventional and jumbo mortgages have higher reserve requirements than government mortgages. Two to six months of your total monthly mortgage payment (PITI) is usually required for most conventional and jumbo mortgages. Government loans will require less, usually one to two months.

Whether or not you are buying a home, reserves are something you should always have.

Real life scenario: Which loan is more likely to be approved for a conventional loan? Borrower A is buying a home for $200,000 with $10,000 for the down payment, has an income of $72,000 a year, credit score of 680, and reserves of $4,000. Borrower B is buying the same home for $200,000 with $10,000 for the down payment, has an income of $72,000 a year, credit score of 650, and reserves of $95,000. While Borrower B's credit score is lower than Borrower A's score, by having significant reserves, lenders are more likely to approve them for a conventional loan.

What is the down payment required to get a mortgage loan?

Underwriting guidelines refer to down payments as the minimum amount of money in percentage terms that you need to bring to closing to qualify for a mortgage. The required down payment is a percentage of the purchase price or appraised value; whichever is lower, you must deposit or bring to closing. Different lending programs and loan types have different down payment requirements. As a general rule, FHA loans require 3.5%, conventional loans require 5%, VA and USDA don't require any, and jumbo loans require between 10% and 30% down depending on the purchase price and size of the mortgage. For example, if you were buying a home with a $200,000 purchase price and appraised value and applying for a conventional loan, you would be required to bring no less than $10,000 to closing. While the above are the general underwriting guidelines, new loan programs for first-time homebuyers have been introduced allowing for conventional financing with a 3% down payment.

The down payment required is different than the money you need to close. In addition to the down payment, there are closing costs associated with your loan. If you do not negotiate the seller to pay the closing costs, you will have to add that amount to the minimum required down payment to qualify for a mortgage. Sellers are allowed to pay between 2% and 6% of the sales price towards borrowers closing costs.

Real life scenario: Let's continue with the $200,000 purchase price example. The estimated closing costs are $3,000. If the seller doesn't pay the closing costs, the money you need to bring to closing for a conventional loan is $13,000 ($10,000 required down payment plus $3,000 in closing costs). However, your realtor and originator will most likely advise you to negotiate the seller to pay your closing costs. You and the seller agree to a sales price of $203,000 with the seller paying $3,000 towards your closing costs. The seller receives the same amount from closing. Now, you will only be required to bring $10,150 to closing (5% of the $203,000 purchase price). Your loan will be $192,850 instead of $190,000.

What is Private Mortgage Insurance (PMI) and how does it affect a borrower?

Private Mortgage Insurance (PMI) is an insurance policy that protects the lender against losses from a borrower's default. Conventional and jumbo loans usually require PMI when the loan-to-value is greater than 80%. The premium charged is based on the loan-to-value, loan type and size, and a borrower's credit score. On conventional loans, publicly traded insurance companies issue these policies.

Government loans charge funding fees, upfront mortgage insurance premiums, and monthly mortgage insurance premiums. Similar to private mortgage insurance on conventional loans, these fees or insurance premiums protect the lender and U.S. government against loss from these higher risk mortgages. These premiums go into a government insurance fund at the Treasury Department to guarantee or insure government mortgages.

The benefit of mortgage insurance to the borrower is that it allows them to obtain a mortgage with less than 20% down payment or equity. The negative is that the premiums add to the monthly payment. Remember, this payment goes to the insurance company or government insurance fund and will not go towards paying your principal or interest requirements.

While mortgage insurance premiums on FHA loans remain on for the life of the loan, PMI can be removed from your payment on conventional mortgages with borrower paid insurance when you reach 78%-80% loan-to-value. Lenders are required by law to terminate PMI when the loan balance is scheduled to reach 78% of your original value of the home or purchase price depending on whichever is lower as long as you are current on the loan. Depending on the terms of your loan and the amortization schedule, this process usually takes between eight and twelve years. Making additional principal payments or property values improving will not remove private mortgage insurance. You can request the lender to remove the mortgage insurance, however, they could say no. More often, PMI is removed through the refinancing of your loan after a few years, assuming the property value has increased.

For conventional loans, either the borrower or the lender can pay the private mortgage insurance premium. When the lender pays the premium, they do so by slightly increasing your rate. Even with the higher rate, the total monthly payment is usually less than when the borrower pays the premium separately. This lender paid option is an excellent solution and should be considered. The negative for the lender paid option is that the borrower cannot cancel the premiums.

A popular strategy to avoid PMI on conventional mortgages with less than a 20% down payment is by taking out two mortgages, sometimes called a piggyback loan. The first mortgage is usually at 80% loan-to-value with a second mortgage for the remaining 5%-15%. While you have two mortgage payments instead of one, and the rate on the second mortgage is probably higher than the first mortgage, you would have a lower total monthly mortgage payment with this strategy.

What is loan-to-value (LTV) and why is it important?

Loan-to-value is a percentage/ratio between the loan amount and the value of your home. To determine the LTV, your lender will divide your loan amount by the lesser of the home's appraised value or purchase price (if applicable).

Your LTV is important to the lender as they underwrite your file. This is because borrowers with more equity in their home are less likely to default on their mortgage. Even if they did default, the bank could take back the property through foreclosure and be able to liquidate with little or no loss. As a rule, the lower the LTV, the lower the interest rate you can obtain will be.

Your LTV could also affect your monthly payment. Remember, private mortgage insurance is usually required on loans with a LTV greater than 80%. The monthly insurance premium is added to your payment and goes directly to the insurance company or fund providing the insurance.

What is debt-to-income ratio (DTI or D/R) and why is it important?

The debt-to-income ratio (DTI) also known as debt ratio (D/R) is the percentage of your gross monthly income that goes towards paying your mortgage and monthly debts. Gross monthly income is the income you earn before taxes are taken out.

The monthly debts that are included in the DTI calculation include your mortgage, auto loans, student loans, credit card payments, personal and finance company loans, 401(k) loans, child support and alimony. Monthly payments for your cable, phone, and utilities are not included in your debt ratio.

The DTI ratio is further broken down into two separate calculations. The front-end ratio is calculated by dividing your entire monthly mortgage payment (principal, interest, taxes, insurance, and when applicable, mortgage insurance, homeowners association fees, and/or condo dues) by your gross monthly income. Lending guidelines usually require this percentage to be at or less than 30%. The back-end ratio is calculated by adding the monthly payments for all the other debt with your mortgage payment. This total is then divided by your gross monthly income. Ideally, the back-end ratio will be at or less than 40%. While these ratios provide a general guideline, exceptions are made based on the strength of the loan application. They will vary based on the loan program applied for.

The DTI is extremely important. Lenders use this to assess the risk of default. As a rule, the lower your debt-to-income ratio, the lower the interest rate will be. Remember, just because you qualify for a larger home and mortgage doesn't mean you should buy it.

Why does it matter what type of property you own or purchase?

The old adage about location, location, and location are the three most important criteria to consider when purchasing a property is only partly true. The type of property you purchase will also affect the resale value and ability to obtain financing. For example, some unique property types like non-warrantable condos, log homes, or manufactured housing have underwriting restrictions that make obtaining a conventional or government mortgage difficult. Therefore, your costs to finance the property will be more expensive and your ability to resell the property in the future may be challenging. Consult with an experienced mortgage and real estate professional prior to making an offer on a unique property.

How does being self-employed affect my ability to get a mortgage?

Being self-employed can make obtaining a mortgage in the conventional or government markets more difficult than salaried employees. Most lenders require you to be in business for two or more years and will review your personal and business tax returns for the last two years to qualify you for the mortgage. Federal underwriting laws require the lender to verify your ability to make your payments and have a maximum debt ratio to be a qualified mortgage. Lenders are discouraged from funding unqualified mortgages.

Businesses and individuals that expense a significant portion of their income may have a difficult time qualifying for a mortgage or obtaining the best rate in the marketplace because their debt-to-income ratio is too high. However, as the economy and housing markets improve, additional lending programs to this market segment will become available.

What is the difference between an owner-occupied, second home, and investment property?

An owner-occupied property is also known as your primary residence. This is the property where you live or intend to live at the entire or majority of the year. A second home is another residential real estate property that you own; however, you do not stay there the majority of time and you don't rent the property out for income. Second homes are often called vacation homes. Investment properties are also called non-owner occupied properties. These properties are owned for the expected return on investment coming from monthly rents and property appreciation.

The underwriting rules are different for each of these ownership types because the risk of default is different. You are least likely to miss a payment on your primary residence, followed by your second home, and then your investment property. Additionally, primary residences are traditionally cared for better than second homes and investment properties. Therefore, lenders charge higher rates and require larger down payments on investment properties.

When you are asked questions, respond with complete honesty. Withholding pertinent information may cause considerable damage later.

—5—

ADDITIONAL MORTGAGE OPTIONS

While the majority, currently estimated at over 85%, of mortgages originated are conventional, FHA, or VA mortgages, there are alternative mortgage products in the marketplace available to you. Some of the additional programs are reverse mortgages, second mortgages, home equity lines of credit (HELOC), hard money, private money, non-conforming mortgages, commercial mortgages, and construction loans. In this chapter, we will examine the benefits and risks of these products to you.

These alternative products are available to meet the needs of clients. Borrower's may pursue an alternative mortgage because they don't meet rigorous underwriting guidelines, they need to close a loan quickly, they want to access the equity in their home without refinancing their first mortgage, they own a residential property(s) in an LLC or company, they want to build a home, or they don't want to have any mortgage payments.

What is a reverse mortgage and how does it work?

A reverse mortgage is a loan program that allows you to convert part of the equity in your home into a monthly payment or line of credit from the lender. In traditional mortgages, you make payments to the lender whereas in a reverse mortgage you receive money from the lender.

Reverse mortgages are restricted to individuals 62 years old or older. The main benefits to reverse mortgages are that they can pay off your current mortgage and require no further monthly payments, supplement your retirement income, or to pay for healthcare costs and other debts. The mortgage is repaid if you refinance it, when you die, sell your home, or when you no longer live in the home as your primary residence.

Reverse mortgages are easier to qualify for as there are no income restrictions or qualifications. Lenders use mathematical calculations based on your age, the type of reverse mortgage applied for, the current interest rates, and the appraised value of your property to determine the maximum loan amount you can qualify for. As a general rule, that number is your age minus 10. For example, if you are 70 years old and your property is worth

Taking time to consult with your financial advisor is recommended.

$300,000, the maximum loan amount you would qualify for is $180,000.

$$70 - 10 = 60 \rightarrow .60 \text{ x } \$300,000 = \$180,000$$

Before you can apply for most reverse mortgages, you must speak or meet with an independently approved housing counseling agency. The agency's responsibility is to explain the loan's costs, financial implications of your decisions, and alternative funding options. The biggest negative to a reverse mortgage is the costs associated with obtaining one. Lenders generally charge an origination fee. There is a mortgage insurance premium required on federally insured reverse mortgages (the most popular product), along with other standard closing costs.

Additionally, it is important to understand that your mortgage balance (amount owed) will increase each month as interest charges accrue or additional advances are taken. Because you retain ownership to your home, you are still required to pay your property taxes, utilities, maintenance, homeowner's insurance, and other expenses. These items are not accounted for in the loan.

What is a second mortgage? What is the difference between a second mortgage and a home equity line of credit?

Second mortgages are mortgages that are in second lien position on title behind a first mortgage. Second mortgages are riskier to a lender and generally have tougher underwriting requirements (credit scores and income) and higher interest rates than a first mortgage. This is due to the fact that if the borrower defaults on any of their mortgages or property taxes and a foreclosure results, the first mortgage lender gets paid their money prior to the second mortgage lender.

Just because they do the job doesn't mean they are great at it. Make sure you are comfortable with the level of expertise you are provided.

In a purchase transaction, a second mortgage can be used to avoid private mortgage insurance or to assist with the down payment requirements. In a refinance, second mortgages can use the equity in your home to pay off credit cards, pay for their child's college education, home improvement projects, or just about anything else you want. Lenders typically require you to own your property for at least one year before tapping into the equity in a refinance.

Second mortgages are usually structured as a loan or as a line of credit, commonly referred to as a home equity line of credit (HELOC). A loan will have a specific loan amount, rate, term, and payment. Rates are usually fixed and terms often range from 10-30 years. A HELOC will be similar to a credit card. It will have a high credit limit and a variable-rate usually tied to the prime rate. You have a minimum payment due based on the amount borrowed and the applicable rate (index plus a banks margin). The prime rate is the most common index used for HELOC's.

HELOC's are more popular than amortizing second mortgages. This is because they have lower monthly payments, minimal or no fees to obtain, and provide greater flexibility to you in regards to borrowing and repaying the loan. The negatives of the HELOC's are that the rates are variable. This isn't bad in a low or falling rate environment; however, when rates are rising, the payments will increase. Another challenge with HELOC's is that lenders may freeze these accounts. It was common during the recent housing crisis in 2008 that lenders were calling due or freezing the home equity line of credit as property values were decreasing. In fact, the ability to obtain a second mortgage in today's marketplace is still difficult. However, as property values continue to increase and economic conditions improve, these products will probably become widely available again.

What are hard money, private money, and non-conforming mortgages?

Hard money, private money, and non-conforming mortgages are loans provided to individuals who may not meet the underwriting guidelines needed to secure a mortgage in the conventional or government marketplace. Private individuals or companies typically provide hard and private money loans, whereas banks or mortgage lenders often provide non-conforming mortgages. These loans usually have higher rates and fees to offset the risk of default to the lender.

The primary reasons borrowers don't qualify for traditional financing are:

1. A borrower(s) credit history and scores are below guidelines.

101

2. A borrower(s) income does not meet guidelines.
3. The property is unique and does not meet guidelines.
4. The property needs repairs or improvements.
5. A borrower owns multiple investment properties.
6. The loan amount exceeds lending limits.

Hard and private money loans are usually short-term solutions to overcome one of the issues above. Many hard or private money mortgages are required to be paid off within 1-3 years, have double-digit interest rates, and cost between three and six origination points. Each origination point represents 1% of the mortgage loan. Therefore, a $100,000 loan with five origination points would mean the origination fee would be $5,000.

Many real estate investors use hard or private money to purchase investment properties to fix and flip. The investor will buy a property in need of improvements, repair it to neighborhood and lending standards, and then sell it in a short period of time, usually less than a year.

When you are purchasing real estate, you should check the properties chain of title for the last three to five years. This will let you know the sequence of transfers and any recent sales on the property. If the property was sold within the last 12 months at a price much less than the current asking price, you need to find out what

Be aware of your responsibilities in the process. Don't go for the short-term fix just to get what you want.

changed? If there were significant improvements made to the property, ask for a detailed list and check with the better business bureau and public records for any complaints on the owner.

Warning: One reason for the recent housing crash resulted from investors who were "flipping" houses. Some investors were taking short cuts on needed repairs to increase profitability. When you buy an existing home, we strongly suggest you get a home inspection. Home inspections are usually done after you sign a purchase contract with the seller and before you move forward with your mortgage application. Inspections cost the buyer between $250 and $600; however, they can limit the risk you will incur on a major repair expense in the near future. The inspector will thoroughly examine the entire home and give you a report on its condition. At this time, you can go back to the seller and negotiate to have these problems resolved prior to closing on the loan. If you and the seller don't agree, then the purchase contract is void. Another way to avoid costly repairs when you buy a home is by negotiating the seller to provide you with a home warranty.

Prior to the crash of 2008, the non-conforming mortgage marketplace was substantial. These lenders provided access to capital for individuals with lower credit scores, higher debt ratios, little to no down payment, or had income challenges from being self-employed. Since the crash, regulatory restrictions have made it extremely difficult and expensive for lenders to fund loans to these borrowers. However, as the housing market and property values are improving, some of the non-conforming products, especially for high credit score borrowers, are starting to come back. The rates on these loans are usually 1%-5% higher than the conventional marketplace.

Jumbo mortgages are considered non-conforming because their loan size exceeds the loan limits set by Fannie Mae and Freddie Mac. However, jumbo borrowers and products are very similar to conventional mortgages with the exception that rates tend to be about .25%-1% higher, loan to values are lower, and adjustable rates are primarily offered. The jumbo mortgage market is fairly strong.

What is a commercial mortgage on a residential property?

When most people think of commercial mortgages, they probably think of a loan on a multi-family apartment building, shopping center, office building, industrial property, or other commercial building. While all these are commercial properties and qualify for a commercial mortgage, *Mortgage Secrets, Strategies & Warnings* addresses residential properties and the mortgages options that are used in the marketplace to finance them. Remember, residential real estate is described as single family residences, two to four unit properties, condos, townhomes, planned unit developments (PUDs), mobile, or manufactured homes.

The most common reason for borrowers to obtain a commercial mortgage on a residential property is when they are buying or refinancing real estate in a limited liability company (LLC) or other legal company for investment purposes. Real estate investors use the LLC or company to protect themselves and their personal assets from any liabilities that may arise from the investment

104

property. Many hard-money lenders will only fund mortgages on investment properties and require the borrower be an LLC.

The other primary use of commercial mortgages on residential investment properties is through the use of "blanket" mortgages. A blanket mortgage is one mortgage that is secured by two or more real properties. Real estate investors who buy and hold multiple residential rental properties often use a "blanket" mortgage. They will collect multiple rents, but only have to pay one mortgage payment. Blanket loans are popular with builders and developers who buy multiple parcels of undeveloped land or a tract of land and then subdivide it into many smaller parcels. When the parcel is sold, whether developed or undeveloped, a portion of the funds will go towards the mortgage balance, the lien against that parcel will be released, and the remaining mortgage balance will stay intact. The same process applies to the real estate investor who may sell one of the rental properties in his blanket mortgage.

The fundamental difference in underwriting residential and commercial mortgages has to deal with income. For residential mortgages, the borrower's income is used to calculate their debt ratio. For commercial mortgages, the properties cash flow, specifically the net operating income, is used to calculate the debt service coverage ratio. These ratios must fall within the lenders guidelines in order to qualify for the mortgage.

Commercial mortgages are considered more risky than residential mortgages. Therefore, the down payments are usually higher, the loan terms often have adjustable rates or balloon payments, and include pre-payment penalties.

What is a construction loan?

Construction loans are used to finance the construction of real estate. In the residential marketplace, the builder or the homeowner will obtain a construction loan to finance building the new property. The most common practice in the marketplace is when the builder obtains the funds from a commercial loan or line of credit they have established with their bank to build the home. The builder may sell you an existing home that has already been built with no specific buyer in mind known as a "spec" home or build a home for you based on your plans and goals. With the second option, the builder will start the construction process after you have been pre-approved for the anticipated mortgage and they receive the initial deposit.

If you don't understand something, it's not wise to bite your tongue. Ask questions until you have complete clarity.

The pre-approval process for a new build home is the same as when you are purchasing a previously owned home. The biggest difference is that your mortgage won't close until the home is 100% complete and a certificate of occupancy has been issued. It is incredibly important for you to realize that any negative changes in your income or credit could cause your loan to be declined and you to lose your initial deposit. The other risk is what the interest rates will be when the home is complete and whether you will qualify if the rates go up. You should have the opportunity to lock your rate for the time needed to build the home, however there may be significant costs associated with long-term rate locks.

When you obtain a construction loan, there will be two phases in the loan process. In the first phase, you essentially get approved for a line of credit to build the home. The bank will release funds to the builder based on a predetermined completion and draw schedule. The second phase of the loan process is when the property is completely built and you obtain or convert to a permanent mortgage. The permanent mortgage may be a fixed or variable-rate and closed under conventional, government, or non-conforming mortgage guidelines.

Your construction loan will either be a one-time close or two-time close process. A one-time close construction loan is when the borrower receives the construction loan and permanent loan approval from the same bank. The benefit is that you will only have to get approved through underwriting one time and incur closing costs once. The negative is that the permanent mortgage products may be limited and the rates may be slightly higher than the market rate.

In a two-time close, you close once on the initial construction loan and again for the permanent mortgage. Typically, it is accomplished with two separate lenders. The negatives are that you incur two sets of closing costs and go through the underwriting process both times. The benefit of a two time close loan is that the permanent financing options may be better than what is available from a one-time close lender.

A key point when you obtain a construction loan is that you are responsible for making monthly payments on the loan while the home is being built. The payments are usually interest-only based on a variable-rate and the loan balance. When the builder obtains the construction loan, you do not make any payments until you take ownership. The builder will calculate the cost of capital and factor this into the cost to build the home.

Warning: When considering any of these additional mortgage options, work with an originator that has experience with closing the specific type of loan desired. With the exception of second mortgages and home equity lines of credit, these products have many unique features and procedures. Inexperienced originators may have difficulty providing you with the best mortgage solution in the marketplace, won't be able to explain the details of the mortgage properly, or know how to effectively process and close the transaction in a timely manner.

—6—

STRATEGIES TO NEGOTIATING A GREAT MORTGAGE

When you are negotiating a mortgage, there are three major variables you should focus on when choosing an originator to work with. The order of importance for the top three may be different depending on your personal needs and goals. The three major variables are:

1. Rate offered
2. Fees charged
3. Service (the ability to close your loan timely and professionally)

In addition, there are two other key variables to consider:

1. Mortgage products and programs available
2. Experience and ethics of the mortgage originator and company

Warning: The challenging part is that originators may not accurately represent their offer or the company's ability to close a loan when you are negotiating a loan with them. For example, it is virtually impossible for a lender to be able to offer the best rate, lowest fees, and the fastest service, yet many make this claim. Think about it logically, if the lender has the lowest rates or fees, they would receive a significant amount of business and their service levels will suffer. Secondly, if an originator offers you the lowest fees and a "no closing cost" mortgage, they do so by increasing the rate to cover the actual closing costs with the additional revenue they receive for selling a higher rate. The marketplace is too competitive for lenders or originators to offer you both the lowest fees and rates on most products.

Similar to you looking to work with a professional you can trust, it is important that you are upfront and honest with your originator. Lying on your application, omitting relevant information, misrepresenting your income, credit worthiness, or other financial information will only lead to delays and problems. The biggest mistake you can make is to think the lender will not find out. Your entire application, credit file, income, and financial information will go through a fraud check as part of the underwriting process. Providing false information will cause your file to be declined and "red flagged" within the mortgage industry database.

This could have serious consequences now and in the future.

Strategy to negotiating a mortgage from a position of strength:

Step 1 – Improve your credit score prior to applying for a mortgage: The higher your credit score, the more options you will have and the lower your rate will be. Review the information in Chapter 2 as needed.

Step 2 – Educate yourself on the mortgage process: Reading *Mortgage Secrets, Strategies, & Warnings* or similar unbiased information will help you know if you are working with a mortgage originator that you can trust.

Step 3 – Put together all of your financial documentation: Make it easy for the originator to do business with you. When they recognize that you're educated in the mortgage process and prepared to close your loan quickly, they are more likely to offer you their best terms.

Step 4 – Determine what is the ideal mortgage program for you: Your originator should find out more about your goals and financial condition before throwing out loan options. They should explain the pros and cons between fixed and adjustable rates along with conventional, government, non-conforming, or other loan programs you qualify for.

Step 5 – Review multiple offers: We strongly suggest you receive a quote, which includes a Good Faith Estimate and Truth-in-Lending from two or three different originators. You want to focus on the following:

1. What is the interest rate and Annual Percentage Rate (APR)? When comparing two similar offers under the same loan program, the one with the lower APR is usually better for the borrower. The exception is for adjustable-rate mortgages where APR's can be manipulated.
2. What are the origination fees and closing costs? Pay attention to all the fees for your loan. The common fees charged on a loan are origination, processing, underwriting, appraisal, credit report, closing, title search, title insurance, and recording. These fees vary based on the originator, lender, and third-party providers.

Step 6 – Be fearless: Don't fall for aggressive sales tactics that focus on emotions. The primary emotion sales people focus on will be fear of losing a great rate. Remember, in the short-term, less than 90 days, nobody knows whether rates are going to go up or down. Rates will change daily based on economic, social, and political conditions domestically and internationally. If the originator misrepresents facts or uses aggressive sale tactics in the beginning of the process, find another company and originator to do business with.

Step 7 – Research the originator and company: You can find out how experienced the originator and company are by reviewing the Nationwide Mortgage Licensing System & Registry (NMLS) www.nmlsconsumeraccess.org. Additionally, you can check the Better Business Bureau (BBB) and consumer rating services to see if there is a pattern of complaints or how others feel about the originator and the company. Ask questions to make sure the originator and company are experienced in the loan products you are applying for.

Step 8 – Ask about service and closing expectations: Service may be the most important of the three key variables (rate, fees, and service). There is significant value in working with an experienced and ethical originator who has the ability to properly explain the loan terms and application process, knowledge on how to structure the loan properly, and meet the timelines for closing your loan.

The challenge is determining what the level of service will be from an originator that you haven't worked with previously. Almost every originator will say they offer excellent service to get you to apply with them, but many can't or won't deliver on their promises. However, if you ask the right questions you can gauge the ethics of the originator and whether on not they can effectively accomplish the task. Some of the questions you can ask are:

1. How quickly can you close my loan or do you guarantee on-time closings?

If the originator tells you they can close your loan in less than two weeks, be careful. While there are exceptions to everything, most mortgages close between 25 and 45 days. Market conditions, lender's underwriting and closing infrastructure, and the originators completeness in the application and processing of the loan file will determine how quickly you can close the loan.

If the originator can't close on time, this could mean extra costs and problems for you. This includes:

- Loss of your down payment and opportunity to purchase the home you had a contract on.
- Increase in the interest rates if your lock expires.
- Additional expenses (movers, storage, lodging) if you are required to exit your current residence.
- Stress and disruptions from day-to-day activities and employment.

2. When can I lock my rate? How long will the rate be locked?

Find out what the company policy is on locking rates. It is common in the marketplace that rates can't be locked until a complete application package from you is in their office, which may or may not include an appraisal. Since rates change daily, be careful of the originators who quote low rates to get the application and appraisal ordered and then increase the rate, even though the market didn't change significantly. Additionally, be careful if you are required to lock for 60-90 days. This can be a sign that the service levels are slow.

3. How will the processing and underwriting of my loan be handled?

While the processor and underwriter are behind the scenes, they play a major part in the level of service you receive. Find out who will be providing these services for you, their experience, and their ability to close your loan application in a timely manner.

Step 9 – Negotiate over the phone or Internet with facts and logic: If you want to meet the originator, do so after receiving their "best" deal. They know the mortgage marketplace is competitive and that they need to work hard and ethically to earn your business. When you are in the originator's office, you are more likely to make a decision based on emotion. Remember, emotional decisions usually favor the originator; logical decisions typically favor you. When you negotiate over the phone or Internet, you are in control of your time and can logically evaluate your options.

The strategy we recommend for negotiating a mortgage is similar to negotiating the purchase of a car. Take the emotion out of the transaction and use logic. When you negotiate in the dealer's showroom, you're excited about the shiny car and everything positive that comes with it. The salesperson is not afraid of losing your business to the competition because you are at their dealership. The dealer may not give you their best price unless you get up and walk out the door.

Real life scenario: When I was in college and selling cars, I remember my manager telling me on multiple occasions, "This is the best deal they are getting. However, if they get up and walk out the showroom, catch them before they get to their car and drive away. I'll come in and figure out how to save the deal." Usually, the client ending up paying a little more for the car then they could have.

Bottom line, you are more likely to get a lower rate and fees by negotiating over the phone or

Internet where you can review the facts and logically make the best decision.

Step 10 – Work with the originator that has the best combination of rate, fees, and service for your goals: Remember, originators can't be the best at all three so determine what is the most important to you. Then work with the originator that can meet your goals, is transparent and trustworthy, has low fees, and competitive rates.

Now that you have a strategy for negotiating a mortgage, the next step is to review quotes from multiple originators. We'd recommend you start with an originator that did a great job for you previously or a referral from a financial professional, realtor, family member, or friend. Additionally, you can contact your current mortgage lender, bank, or credit union. If you aren't confident in these resources and want additional offers, you can apply online, respond to recent marketing you've been exposed to, or solicitations you've received.

It still may be difficult to know who to trust and which offers are legitimate. Therefore, in the next few chapters, we will dispel some of the secret sales tactics within the mortgage industry and warn you about what could go wrong with your loan application.

—7—

SECRETS LENDERS AND ORIGINATORS DON'T WANT YOU TO KNOW

If it sounds too good to be true, it usually is. This chapter will educate you on some of the secrets about sales that you should be aware of in the mortgage marketplace. Many times, the sales practices are intended to confuse you or make their product or service sound special. In reality, this is covering up a way to charge you higher rates or fees.

Secret #1 – If you don't apply now, you may never be able to get this rate again: Mortgage originators and lenders don't know whether the rates are going to go up or come down from day-to-day. Mortgage rates are heavily influenced by the yield on the 10-year Treasury security. This index is affected by economic conditions in the United States and abroad, political turmoil in the world, the stock market, and a host of other factors. Rates change daily and when there is extreme volatility in the marketplace, they may change several times each day.

Secret #2 – If you apply with a specific mortgage originator, they can magically improve your credit scores and get you a better rate: While it is true that a higher score will help you get approved for a mortgage at a lower interest rate, there is no magic or quick fix. Some originators try to convince you that they have some inside connection or secret strategy to remove legitimate negative items from your credit report. There is no secret, just fundamentals and strategies that you can follow in Chapter 2.

Secret #3 – If you set up a bi-weekly payment plan, you will get a better mortgage and save thousands of dollars over the life of your loan: This is partially correct. You will pay off your loan quicker because you are making an extra payment each year. A bi-weekly payment plan will not affect the rate you qualify for. Some originators will use a software program to show the effect of bi-weekly payments in an effort to deflect your focus from the higher interest rate they are offering you. Don't get caught up in these charts, negotiate the best rate and fees.

A bi-weekly payment plan is simple. Your monthly mortgage payment is divided in half and collected every two weeks. Since there are 52 weeks in a year, there are 26 payments collected, which is the same as making 13 monthly mortgage payments. Paying additional on your principal will save you money by paying less interest on your mortgage, reduce the term of your mortgage, and increase the equity in your home at a faster rate.

If you want to set up the bi-weekly payment system, do so with the lender you make your mortgage payments to after the loan closes. If the servicing lender does not allow for bi-weekly payments, you can simply add principal to your monthly payments or make an additional payment each year. Be cautious about using a third party service that will charge you a set-up fee and then monthly transaction fees. These costs reduce the benefit and are often shared with the originator.

Secret #4 - If you refinance with a specific originator, you can "skip" two mortgage payments: While this sounds great and if structured properly you will not have to make a mortgage payment for two months, you're not skipping anything. You still owe the mortgage interest and may incur a late fee on the existing mortgage. Furthermore, if there is something that prohibits the new loan from closing and you don't instantaneously pay the current payment due, the result may be a late payment and your inability to refinance at the best rate in the immediate future.

Continue to handle your responsibilities as usual until the process is complete. Don't take an unnecessary risk.

Typically when you refinance, you skip one payment because mortgage payments are due in arrears (at the end of the month, unlike rent, which is due at the beginning of the month). Let's say you close on Tuesday, January 15th. Your loan will fund on Monday, January 21st, after the three day right of rescission expires. Your new lender will charge you 11 days of interim interest from the January 21st through the 31st, so that they can make your payments due on the 1st of each month. In the above case, your first payment is due March 1st. You will be "skipping" the mortgage payment for February.

Your payoff on the original loan will be higher than your principal balance. Assuming you made all of your payments on time on the above refinance, your payoff is the principal balance along with the interest through the 21st or the date the lender receives the funds to pay off your existing loan, whichever is later.

Here is how you can "skip" two mortgage payments. Using the above example, if you don't make your January 1st payment and you close on the 15th, you won't make a mortgage payment January or February. However, your payoff will include the January payment and a late fee for the lender not receiving your payment by the 15th, plus the interest through January 21st.

The other way to skip two payments would be to wait to close your refinance until the last couple days of the month, thereby the loan will fund in the following month. For example, instead of closing on January 15th, you close on January 29th. The refinance would fund on Monday February 4th. The lender collects 25 days of interest, from the 4th through the 28th, and your first payment is due April 1st. You skipped the mortgage payments for February and March, however you did incur interest charges throughout the process.

Warning: While this sounds good and something every originator can coordinate, you need to proceed with caution. If things go wrong and you do not close your loan as planned, you could incur late fees or a 30-day late payment on your credit report. This would significantly damage your credit and may prohibit you from being able to refinance. Remember fundamental #1 from Chapter 1; continue making all of your payments. If you have an existing FHA mortgage, you do not want to use the second method to skip two payments as you will incur an extra month of interest. FHA payoffs incur interest charges through the end of the month they receive the payoff, not the date the funds are received by the lender like other mortgages.

Secret #5 – If you close a loan with their mortgage company, there won't be any fees "no closing costs" and they still have the "best" rates: It is impossible to close a first mortgage loan without fees or closing costs being *incurred*. However, the originator can structure the loan so that those costs are covered for you. This is done by offering you a higher interest rate and using the additional revenue received from the lender to pay the actual fees.

This is a good strategy for you to consider when obtaining a mortgage. Just know that the marketplace is too competitive for lenders or originators to offer you both the lowest fees and rates on most mortgage products.

Secret #6 – If you work with their mortgage company, the originator promises your home will appraise at the value needed to close your loan: Originators can't guarantee what value your home will appraise at, nor can they induce the appraiser to "hit" a specific value needed. Due to the previous challenges in the marketplace where lenders and originators influenced appraisers, appraisals are now ordered through appraisal management companies.

Appraisal management companies are in business to manage the process of having an appraisal completed. This includes accepting orders from originators, recruiting and contracting licensed appraisers to perform the appraisal, and review and verify the work of the appraiser. While this process has added to the cost of appraisals to you, the quality and reliability of the reports have improved.

Secret #7 – If you close at the end of the month, your closing costs will be lower: Your closing costs will not change based on the date of the month you close your loan, the prepaid interest changes. Prepaid interest is not a closing costs, it is the interest from the closing or funding date through the end of the month to set your monthly payment due the 1st of each month. Closing a purchase loan near the end of a month allows you to bring less money to settlement because there is less prepaid interest.

Warning: Be careful when you review multiple loan proposals and good faith estimates (GFE's). Originators may not accurately represent the prepaid items in an effort to make their loan payment and terms appear better. The primary prepaid items you have are prepaid interest, real estate taxes put into an escrow account, and homeowners insurance paid into an escrow account.

Secret #8 – If you want to use the equity in your home to consolidate your debts, you need to refinance your first mortgage: While refinancing your existing first mortgage and credit cards into one new mortgage and payment may accomplish your goals, it may not be your best solution. You need to take into account the closing costs, rates, and other loan options available to you. If you have a low fixed-rate first mortgage and want to access the equity in your home, we strongly suggest you look into a home equity line of credit (HELOC) or personal loan.

Warning: Many mortgage originators will only recommend refinancing your existing mortgage(s) and credit cards into a new first mortgage. The reason is because this is the only solution they have where they can earn income or where they will make the largest fee. This is not what is in your best interest.

There is one final secret I want to leave you with that lenders or originators may not share with you.

Secret #9 – Paying cash can save you thousands in closing costs: When you are buying real estate, if you can pay cash and not take out a mortgage, you should strongly consider this strategy. Your ability to negotiate a lower price with the seller is greatly increased, as they don't have to wait for your loan to go through the application, underwriting, and closing process or worry if you'll be approved for the mortgage altogether. Additionally, your closing costs and the stress of the mortgage process will be minimal.

If you decide you'd prefer to have a mortgage on the property in the future, the process is simple. Follow the advice in this book and work with a professional that you trust. If you would have been approved when you made the offer to purchase the property and there hasn't been any significant change to your income or credit, you'll be approved later.

Before you decide on which strategy to pursue, you will want to check with your accountant regarding the tax benefits of having a mortgage on the property. Furthermore, you'll want to look at the opportunity costs of using your cash to buy the real estate versus taking out a mortgage and investing that money elsewhere.

There are a few reasons why they say, "Cash is king" when buying real estate. Typically, you can negotiate a lower price or get the seller to accept your offer. More importantly, when paying cash, you avoid the many surprises the mortgage process can throw at you.

In conclusion, by revealing some of the secret sales tactics originators use in the application process, you can make a better decision on their ethics and whether or not you want to work with them.

—8—

WARNINGS!
HOW TO AVOID SURPRISES
AND BE PREPARED FOR WHAT
CAN GO WRONG WITH YOUR
APPLICATION

There is a reason why our number one fundamental to borrowing money is to continue making all of your payments. Simply put, there are so many things that can go wrong between the application and closing of a mortgage. This chapter will address the most common surprises that cause problems with your loan application. If you understand these issues in advance, you can be better prepared to overcome any obstacles that come up. Many of these can be avoided altogether if your lender or originator does a great job on the initial application and processing of your loan file. You need to be forthright with your situation and provide all of the required documentation in a timely manner. There are occasions when surprises in the process are beyond the originator or your control. There are many third party providers that are delivering services that need to be coordinated to make the process go smoothly.

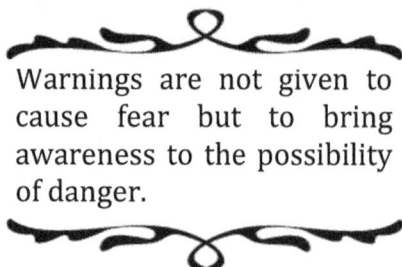

> Warnings are not given to cause fear but to bring awareness to the possibility of danger.

The lender and their underwriter will play a critical part to the mortgage transaction. Some have very conservative underwriting standards while others are aggressive. Additionally, some lenders focus on being a leader in underwriting turn times and support, while others are slow and methodical. Ideally, you will want to work with the platform that meets your goals and needs. Regardless of what their infrastructure or risk tolerance is they all focus on the primary underwriting areas of credit, capacity, and collateral. It's important that we address many of the items that can go wrong with an application in these areas.

There are many surprises involving your credit. Some of them occur prior to the application, while others happen after the initial application. The solution to avoiding the issues prior to the application is to obtain a copy of your credit report annually or ninety to one hundred and eighty days before you plan on starting the process. A free copy can be obtained from www.annualcreditreport.com.

Some of the credit issues that may surprise you prior to the application are:

- Your credit score is lower than you expected.
- You recently maxed out your credit cards causing your credit score to drop.
- There are late payments on your report from debts you co-signed for.
- Your ex-spouse hasn't refinanced a mortgage or debt that remains on your credit report.
- There are negative items on your credit report that are not yours.

After initial application and preliminary approval, there are credit surprises that can cause delays in your loan or for it to be declined. Some of these are:

- Your lender pulled or required a new or updated credit report and your credit score dropped below the minimum needed to fund the loan.
- You can't prove the primary borrower is paying the loan you co-signed for and it needs to be included in your debt ratio. Lenders will require copies of cancelled checks or bank statements for the last 3-12 months to prove the co-signed loan is being paid by the primary borrower.
- There are negative items on your credit report that are yours. However, they should have been removed or updated showing paid.

Unfortunately, you lost your bankruptcy paperwork or other documentation proving the debt has been satisfied.

A great number of surprises come in the area of your income or capability to make the payments. Many times the originator and underwriter calculate your income differently resulting in your debt ratio to be too high and your loan application to be declined. Other times you will do something that causes the problem. In order to avoid these unexpected scenarios, do not make any major purchases or change jobs before or during the application process. Additionally, provide all of the requested documentation upfront so that your originator can have a better chance of accurately calculating your income. Below is a list of surprises that result when reviewing your capability to make your mortgage payment.

- You changed your job and forgot to let the originator and lender know.
- You made a major purchase during the application process and no longer qualify.
- The property taxes or home owners insurance are much higher than initially estimated.
- You did not tell the originator about a property you own and have a private mortgage on.
- You haven't filed your tax returns for the last couple of years.
- You have a 401(k) loan and the originator didn't ask and you didn't tell them in the initial application.

- You have child support payments and the originator didn't ask and you didn't tell them on the initial application.
- You receive child support, however it will not continue for three more years.
- Your tax returns show significant losses for a business you own.
- Your tax returns show significant losses for other real estate you own.
- You are a commissioned sales person and wrote off significant business expenses that were not reimbursed.
- Your tax return provided to the originator does not match the transcript the lender obtained from the IRS.
- You have part-time income, but you can't prove a two-year history.
- You are a temporary or contract employee and can't close unless you receive permanent employment.
- You have been self-employed for less than two years.

The surprises in the collateral area can be the most frustrating. This is because they are often beyond your control and you are required to pay a non-refundable fee for the appraisal prior to finding out about the problem. The solution is to work with an originator that will complete the market research needed on your property, review your complete loan file, and pre-approve your application before ordering the appraisal.

Warning: Inexperienced originators and some companies will require you to order an appraisal as soon you apply in an attempt to lock you into working with them. They do not thoroughly review your loan file or the applicable underwriting guidelines. Be cautious when considering working with these companies.

Some of the surprises that happen regarding your collateral (real estate) include:

- The property did not appraise at the value expected or needed to close the transaction.
- The property has repairs that need to be completed prior to closing.
- The property is unacceptable to the underwriter.
- The owner-occupancy level in the condo development does not meet the underwriting guidelines.
- The appraiser can't find comparables on your property that the lender will accept.
- The lender did not accept the appraisal.
- You are purchasing or refinancing a unique property that the lender is not comfortable with.
- The appraisal review significantly cut the value of the original appraisal.
- The appraiser or appraisal review can't be completed in a timely manner.

Another area where surprises come into play when underwriting your file involves verifying the assets you need to close or have listed on your application. Some of the surprises are:

- You can't prove the assets listed on your application.

- Your down payment has not seasoned (funds in your bank account for 90 days) and you can't explain any large deposit(s).
- You're receiving a gift for the down payment; however, you don't provide the needed documentation.
- You own more residential properties than the underwriting guidelines allow for.
- Your bank statements show numerous NSF charges causing the underwriter to decline your loan.

In addition to the underwriting surprises that can cause problems with your loan application there are operational or transactional issues that could complicate your loan closing in a timely manner. Some of the operational or transactional surprises that happen are:

- Verifications of mortgage, rent, income, and/or assets were not sent out by the processor.
- Verifications were sent out, but the verifying source has not completed the documents.
- There are title issues beyond your control that need to be resolved.
- The payoff came in higher than you anticipated.
- The lender changed their underwriting guidelines and you no longer qualify.
- You lost your required income, asset, or legal paperwork.
- Interest rates increased considerably and you no longer qualify or the benefit of refinancing is no longer there.

- The appraisal did not get ordered in a timely manner.
- The application and disclosures were not sent out on time or correctly.
- You did not acknowledge the changes to the application and disclosures.
- The government shuts down and can't verify your tax transcripts.
- A natural disaster occurred (hurricane, flooding, wild fires, tornado, etc.) causing massive damage in your region. The lender will need to verify your property was not damaged.

Congratulations, you made it through the entire underwriting process and you are ready to close. Not so fast. There are still surprises waiting for you. Some of the closing issues that may surprise you are:

- Your name or address was misspelled on the legal paperwork. New closing documents need to be generated and signed.
- The lender is overwhelmed and can't generate the closing documents when you want to close.
- The title company can't close the loan at a convenient time for you.
- You have to leave town for business or personal reasons.
- Your ex-spouse is still on title and isn't cooperating to sign the required paperwork.
- You missed your closing date and thought you could simply sign the paperwork the following day.

- The rates, terms, or fees changed from what you were promised and expecting.
- You spent the down payment money needed to bring to closing.
- You didn't bring certified funds to closing and thought cash or a personal check was acceptable.
- The lender forgot to wire the funds for your loan to the title company, closing agent, or attorney.
- The HUD-1 closing statement wasn't approved by the lender and had mistakes the lender won't accept.
- Your spouse wasn't happy and rescinded the loan.

As you can see, there are a lot of challenges involved with the closing of a mortgage. This is why many people rate service as the most important variable, over the interest rate and closing costs. The originator that can deliver the product needed at the best combination of a low rate, low closing costs, and excellent service is the individual and company you want to do business with.

There is one final warning we want to leave you with. Be cautious of those who tell you that you can purchase real estate with no money down and you will become independently wealthy. Many of those individuals made more money selling CD's and "consulting services" than they made in real estate.

If it doesn't feel right, don't go against your intuition.

Other times they use you to find them properties to invest in, cutting you out of the transaction.

While there are a lot of benefits and opportunities to be successful in real estate, making money with investment properties can be difficult. There are many things that can go wrong and financing for investment properties can be expensive, especially if your credit is less than excellent and you have little down payment. Some of the biggest challenges with investing in real estate are:

- Property values can go down.
- Renters can stop paying their rent.
- Renters can significantly damage the property.
- Home improvement costs may exceed the budget.

When one of these issues happens, we've seen it destroy the individual's credit and financial situation. Before you decide to jump into real estate, make sure you have a plan on how to survive any challenges and the reserves to withstand the surprises.

In conclusion, owning a home and taking out a mortgage is a significant decision. The same way it is recommended that you have a plan to meet your financial goals, you should have a plan for borrowing money. Start by making sure your credit report doesn't have any errors by obtaining a free copy at www.annualcreditreport.com. Then use the knowledge you've learned from *Mortgage Secrets, Strategies, & Warnings* to negotiate a great mortgage.

The information in *Mortgage Secrets, Strategies, & Warnings* is based on the experience and knowledge of the authors. We encourage you do further research or ask questions. If you need legal advice, consult your attorney, If you need tax advice, consult with your CPA or accountant. If you have any questions for Jeff Flees regarding the material in this book, finding a mortgage professional to work with, or need help with a mortgage application, you can send an email to jflees@loanacademymortgage.com or connect through the following company websites.

- Loan Academy:
  www.loan-academy.com
- Loan Academy Mortgage Corporation:
  www.loanacademymortgage.com

ABOUT THE AUTHORS

Jeff Flees is a notable financial professional and entrepreneur with more than 20 years of experience in the mortgage banking and financial services sector. Having owned a mortgage company for over 14 years, he has helped countless consumers realize the dream of home ownership or save money through refinancing their mortgage. Jeff and his companies have originated and funded over fifteen thousand residential mortgages, employed hundreds of originators, and sold or brokered mortgages with the top banks and lending institutions in the United States. He currently holds a mortgage license ID #9735 through the National Mortgage Licensing System and his current company Loan Academy Mortgage Corporation, NMLS ID is #1227256 (www.loanacademymortgage.com).

In addition to his vast knowledge and experience in the residential mortgage marketplace, he owns a commercial and small business finance firm, Loan Academy Commercial Capital www.loan-academycc.com and a mortgage consulting and recruiting firm Loan Academy, www.loan-academy.com.

Jeff's financial career started in college. He was a top college agent for Northwestern Mutual Life selling life insurance and annuities. After graduation, he obtained his Series 7 license and became a financial planner. When opportunities in the mortgage industry presented themselves, he applied the core values and financial planning strategies he learned to the mortgage industry. He is committed to helping consumers and financial professionals make better financial and mortgage decisions.

Marala Scott is a Bestselling Author, Motivational Speaker, Ghostwriter and Oprah's Ambassador of Hope who shares powerful words of inspiration wherever she goes. Marala has shared her unimaginable life story to help others learn to forgive, accept challenges and adapt to changes in life, chronicled in her bestselling memoir, *In Our House: Perception vs. Reality* (an Amazon #3 Best Seller) and Surrounded By Inspiration. Bad to the Bone: The True Story of David Tuccaro Jr. (an Amazon Best Seller) is a heart-wrenching story that inspires you to believe when there is no evidence of hope. Her recent novel, *Intuition*, co-authored with her daughter, Alyssa Curry, is a romantic psychological thriller that teaches why and how to trust your intuition.

Marala speaks from the heart with her life-changing words of faith and strength. Her efforts caught the attention of Oprah Winfrey, who honored her as an Ambassador of Hope in 2009 and stated, "A childhood of abuse almost kept Marala Scott from a life of happiness...until she discovered how to use her story to help others." A widely sought after Motivational Speaker and Ghostwriter at Seraph

Books. She helps share inspiration others have experienced with their power and passion.

Marala shares her perspective on helping others value the power of having truth and transparency in his or her personal life and in business. When you learn to have ethical business practices, you will be able to discern those that do not. For more information about Marala Scott, visit www.maralascott.com.